RESOURCE BANK
Book 2

Dedication
To Rebekah and Rachael, Tom and Grace
and
Laurie with thanks

RESOURCE BANK
Book 2

by Margaret Cooling and Diane Walker
with Maggie Goodwin

British and Foreign Bible Society
Stonehill Green, Westlea, SWINDON SN5 7DG, England

A catalogue record for this book is available from the British Library
ISBN 0 564 08565 0

Printed in Great Britain by Stanley L. Hunt (Printers) Ltd.

Cover design and illustrations by Jane Taylor

Bible Societies exist to provide resources for Bible distribution and use. The British and Foreign Bible Society (BFBS) is a member of the United Bible Societies, an international partnership working in over 180 countries. Their common aim is to reach all people with the Bible, or some part of it, in a language they can understand and at a price they can afford. Parts of the Bible have now been translated into over 1,900 languages. Bible Societies aim to help every church at every point where it uses the Bible. You are invited to share in this work by your prayers and gifts. Bible Society in your country will be very happy to provide details of its activity.

CONTENTS

ACKNOWLEDGEMENTS

The authors gratefully acknowledge the help of Linda Armitt, Ruth Cooper, Karen Edgington and Mabel Lie in the preparation of this manuscript. Our thanks also go to Jean Mead for contributing the activity on page 27, to Sue Hatherly for advice and ideas for music activities, to Gillian Crow for checking certain factual details and to Trevor Cooling for writing the Introduction.

We would also like to thank Dr John Goldingay, Dr Stephen Travis, both of St John's Theological College, Nottingham, Sid Freeman and Helen Thacker for reading and commenting on different parts of the manuscript. Final responsibility for any errors of course lies with the authors alone.

We also wish to thank Elaine Walker and the pupils and staff of the following schools for testing material:

Albany Junior School, Stapleford • Bramcote Church of England (Aided) Primary School, Nottingham • Bramcote Hills Primary School, Nottingham Brambletye Middle School, Surrey • The Manor Primary School, Romford Stevenson Junior School, Stapleford • St. John's Church of England (Controlled) Primary School, Stapleford • St Paul's Church of England (Aided) Primary School, Hereford • Stoneleigh First School, Ewell • William Lilley Infant School, Stapleford

The activity on page 23 is a development of an activity which appears in *Christianity Topic Book 2* (RMEP). The activity on page 26 is a development of an activity which appears in *Assemblies for the Summer Term* (RMEP).

This book has been produced under the auspices of the Stapleford Project.

The Stapleford Project is a curriculum development initiative based at Stapleford House Education Centre. The project aims to produce materials and offer in–service training to support the teaching of Christianity in schools.

Stapleford House Education Centre is the national conference and study centre of the Association of Christian Teachers. Full details of courses and of publications sponsored by the centre are available from: Stapleford House Education Centre, Wesley Place, Stapleford, Nottingham, NG9 8DP

INTRODUCTION

The place of the Bible in primary school religious education

For as long as there has been formal schooling the Bible has found a place in the classroom. However, its effective use in school religious education is an issue which continues to generate controversy, sometimes quite heated.

The history of the use of the Bible

A brief study of the syllabuses appearing after the 1944 Education Act makes it immediately apparent that religious education and teaching the Bible were considered synonymous at the time. The content of the Bible was the one thing that the different Christian denominations who were involved in drawing up these syllabuses could agree on.

However, in the mid–1960s Ronald Goldman published two highly influential studies on children's understanding of the Bible, which seriously undermined teachers' confidence in these syllabuses. His results seemed to show that the Bible was, to put it simply, too difficult for young children to understand. He claimed that it was not a children's book and that they would develop serious misunderstandings if introduced to its complex theological ideas at too young an age.

Confidence in the Bible as a suitable book for primary schools was further damaged by the rejection of the so–called "confessional" approach to religious education with which it was associated. This was based on the assumption of the truth of Christianity and had as its goal the transmission of the Christian faith to children. It was discredited because it was seen as indoctrinatory in that it both ignored other religions and did not allow children the freedom to choose their beliefs for themselves.

The multifaith approach to religious education, which replaced the confessional approach, has, however, also been a major factor in re–establishing confidence in the Bible as an "educational" book in recent years. In this approach it is recognized that sacred texts are central to religion, and educational justice cannot be done if children are not introduced to them. The Bible has been rediscovered as the living book of the Christians, alongside the Qur'an in Islam, the Guru Granth Sahib in Sikhism and so on. This regaining of confidence has been further enhanced by the realization that Goldman's theories do not take enough account of the way in which children learn religious ideas. It is now widely felt that there were some serious shortcomings in his work.

The current use of the Bible in primary schools

Although in theory the Bible has a valid place in modern religious education, the evidence is that it is not used particularly well. The research carried out by Dr Leslie Francis in primary schools in Gloucestershire,[1] and various reports by Her Majesty's Inspectors of Schools indicate that:

(i) Bible stories are often selected at random with little attention being given to their religious message. A widely quoted example of this is where the story of Jesus feeding 5,000 people is used as part of a piece of work designed to persuade children not to drop litter.

(ii) Little guidance is given in schemes of work on criteria for selection of stories, the important religious ideas to be explored or the level at which stories should be approached.

(iii) The range of biblical material taught is so narrow that the same stories are used over and over again and are often presented in an educationally undemanding fashion.

(iv) Little attention is given to the biblical context and background of the stories used.

Ian Birnie captures the situation well when he describes current use as reducing "the Bible to a history book, a book of moral stories and fables or worse still to a source of proof texts for what is claimed to be the Christian faith and life."[2] The ideal that children should appreciate it as the living book of the Christians is rarely attained.

Controversies surrounding the use of the Bible in schools

Although many teachers are including biblical material in their teaching, many also express anxiety about whether they are doing the right thing for their children. There are four particular issues which underlie this anxiety:

1. The Bible is not a child's book

It is here that the continuing influence of Goldman's work is strongest. Basically the fear is that by introducing children to biblical material too early they will develop crude ideas in the order of "God is an old man in the sky". Like the Russian cosmonaut who announced to the world that he had been "there" and not found God, they will reject these when they begin to mature in their thinking. Two things can be said about this.

Firstly, it is a fact that learning in all subjects proceeds by children refining their understanding of concepts. For example, many children have a scientifically crude idea of an atom as a collection of solid balls. However, they do not reject the concept of the atom *per se* as they learn more and realize the mistaken nature of their childhood ideas. Rather, under the guidance of good teaching, they become more refined in their thinking. Likewise, with religion children have many crude ideas. It is true that these are "mistaken" when compared with sophisticated theological thinking, but they are not "mistaken" if by that it is meant that children should never hold such ideas. Indeed it seems likely that such childhood "mistakes" are essential if children are going to be able to develop more sophisticated modes of thought in the future. The role of the teacher is to help children build on their "mistakes" by providing new experiences and opportunities for conversation which encourage them to refine their thinking. We should not underestimate a child's capacity to do this.

Secondly, it is becoming increasingly clear that one of the reasons why children have difficulty in handling biblical material is because it so often makes no sense to them in their own world of experience. Religious ideas have to be related to, or earthed in, children's experience if they are going to be successfully integrated into their patterns of thinking. Otherwise they will be like a proverbial cuckoo chick in amongst their other ideas. As one writer has said about the biblical concept of salvation:

> Pupils are not going to be able to understand salvation until they have learnt what it is to be saved, not in a religious way but in all kinds of other ways — to be saved from drowning by a lifeboat, to save each week and put it in the bank, and to feel safe and tucked up for the night.[3]

In order to assist in this earthing of biblical concepts, we have included ideas for a range of activities that can be used for introducing biblical material into the classroom and have suggested links that can be made with other areas of the curriculum. Part of this process of earthing is also to encourage children to explore and develop their ability to use religious language.[4]

2. The question of miracles

Some people argue that miracle stories are inappropriate for young children. There is clearly a problem if children are encouraged to believe that biblical characters are magicians or that God's action can be invoked as a simple solution to all life's problems. However, the Bible does not treat miracles in this way, but rather places them in a context which conveys a theological message and which thereby gives a broader meaning to the event. For example the relationship of faith is a crucial element of many New Testament miracles. They are not presented as "happenings" for their own sake.

We have included a number of miracle stories in this collection because we believe it would be quite wrong to ignore them. They are part of the biblical world and many modern Christians believe that they actually took place. To exclude them would be to distort the Bible and is not something that is done with the sacred scriptures of other religions when they are used in religious education. It is, however, important that when teaching these stories they are dealt with in the context of a theme which they communicate and are also related to other biblical material which illustrates that theme. Furthermore, as with the miracle stories of other religious traditions, it is important that they are treated as the heritage of particular communities. In the classroom, study of them should be introduced by phrases such as "we are going to listen to a story which is important for Christians", which leave children free either to identify with them or not. If asked whether these stories actually happened, the best answer a teacher can give at this level is that some people believe that they did and others (including some Christians) that they did not.

3. The question of truth

This leads us to consider perhaps one of the most debated issues amongst Christian theologians, whether or not Christian faith depends on the historical accuracy of the Bible. Opinions vary across a spectrum from those who insist that it is literally true at all points, to those who regard questions of historical truth as totally irrelevant to genuine faith. The fact that scholars disagree on this issue means that it is quite wrong for teachers to assume any one position as normative. The problem is that the primary school classroom is clearly not the place for detailed and technical theological discussions. The challenge (and it is a very difficult challenge) is to remain fair to this difference of opinion without making the Bible unusable in the primary school context.

Probably the one thing that most Christians can agree on is that the Bible is not simply a description of a series of events, but is fundamentally a book with a message. In this book we have therefore concentrated on that message. To this end, we have generally taken the text at face value and have not entered into discussions of historicity. This is consistent with the way in which sacred texts from other religions are usually handled in schools. However, it may well be that children ask questions about historical truth. If so it will be important to make them aware both that there is a difference of opinion amongst Christians on this matter and that religious language employs different genres to convey a message, e.g. poetry, symbol, history, metaphor and myth. Analysis of which genre particular texts represent is not, however, the prime purpose of this book.

Some of the stories we use are particularly controversial in this respect, for example Ruth, Jonah, the siege of Jericho and the nature miracles in the New Testament. Here again we have not entered into the archaeological and textual evidence for and against their historicity. In our opinion the amount of information that is needed to make a fair and reasoned judgement is quite substantial and, furthermore, is often difficult to interpret. It simply was not possible to do justice to this in the space available. It also seemed wrong that we should present our conclusions on these debates, with the implication that there are simple answers.

Even putting aside the question of historicity, it is, of course, also true that theologians vigorously debate the question of how biblical texts should be interpreted. Inevitably, therefore, some people will disagree with our description of the message conveyed by certain passages. Again it is unrealistic for teachers in primary schools to introduce pupils to the technicalities of this theological controversy. We have therefore sought to utilize what might be called traditional interpretations, which are widely accepted amongst Christians of many different denominations. Again this is in line with the way in which the sacred texts of other religions are handled in schools. It is, however, important to realize that no book on the Bible will be neutral or objective in the interpretations it adopts. Any such book will inevitably reflect a theology which the authors find convincing. This book is no exception.

4. The relationship with Judaism

A major misunderstanding is created if it is implied that the part of the Bible which Christians call the Old Testament is only a precursor to the New Testament and not also the sacred Scripture of Judaism in its own right. The problem is that there are in fact two ways of interpreting the Old Testament/Hebrew Bible, namely the Christian and the Jewish. Although there is much common ground, sometimes Christians and Jews understand the significance of the same text in different ways. It needs to be clearly understood that in this book we have treated the Old Testament material as part of the Christian Bible. We fully appreciate the sensitivity of this issue and do not want to deny that there is an authentic Jewish treatment of these texts. We do, however, want it to be absolutely clear that in this book we are dealing with the material in its role as part of the Christian Bible.

Of course Christians utilize Jewish insights in their attempt to understand the Old Testament, but it is only honest to make plain that they do this as Christians. The inclusion in this book of practices and ideas from certain Jewish festivals is meant to underline the immense debt of Christianity to Judaism

When it comes to the New Testament there is an important issue to be taken into account. Angela Wood, a Jew and an LEA religious education adviser, paints the problem very starkly in an article where she describes her young daughter's first encounter with the Easter story at her primary school: [5] Ester, came home distraught that "we" (the Jews) should have killed Jesus and were such a horrible people. It has to be accepted that the New Testament does focus on some negative aspects of first–century Judaism. Every religion has its negative side, but it is important that children are not left with the impression that this was the total picture of the Judaism of Jesus' day. The picture needs balancing by ensuring that they are aware that Jesus himself was a Jew, as were most of his early followers, and that there were many noble, honest and God–fearing Jews around in his time. It would be a travesty if religious education were ever unwittingly to fuel anti–semitism. The danger that it might is apparent from Ester's negative feelings about her own people.

Using the Bible in school

Another important point that has to be remembered is that the various authors of the Bible had no idea that it would be used by primary schools some 2,000 or more years later! They wrote with a very different purpose in mind, namely the teaching and edification of the religious community and the announcement of their message to the world. The Bible is proclamation designed to evoke the response of faith in its readers.[6]

This means that using it in schools takes it outside of its "normal" context. The Bible was not written by a teacher as a result of a commission from an educational publisher, nor was it designed to be a quarry of stories for illustrating teaching themes. There is therefore a delicate balance to be maintained between being true to its nature as the "faith–proclaiming", sacred text of the Christian community and using it in a way that is educationally appropriate in the modern school, where belief on the part of the pupils can neither be assumed nor sought. In seeking to achieve this balance we have employed the following principles:

1. Teaching should be true to the meaning of the text
Increasingly the educational importance of teaching structural concepts rather than just passing on information, is being recognized. Thus in an influential

report on religious education it was stated that: "Concepts are the main focal point of any educational programme... concepts help us to make sense of what we observe and encounter in particular religions".[7] The key point is that the purpose of introducing biblical material is to ensure that children come to understand those concepts that are fundamental to the Christian faith and not to provide general knowledge fodder. In using the Bible in this book we have therefore tried to remain true to the underlying concepts that the text conveys. Of course scholars will, in particular cases, disagree as to what the real message is, but we have sought to utilize the consensus within mainstream Christianity. So in grouping biblical material under themes we have tried to make our selection on the basis of the meaning that is central to the text in question.

2. The use of the Bible must support the curriculum

Balanced against the requirement to represent fairly the meaning of the biblical text for Christians, is the need to use it in a way that supports the modern primary school curriculum. We have sought to achieve this in three ways:

Firstly, although we have grouped the passages according to their theological meaning we have used titles which are appropriate to the primary curriculum. For example the biblical idea of "covenant" is included under the heading of "promise", since the former would not figure in the curriculum but the latter often does.

Secondly, in selecting material for inclusion we have tried to reflect the major theological themes of the Bible. However, in certain cases a theme has been given a higher profile than it has in the biblical text, because it has traditionally been important for primary schools. For example the theme of "sharing" is present in the Bible, although it does not have the emphasis given to it in many primary schools. We have therefore included it as one that teachers will be able to utilize. Furthermore we have sometimes used a secondary idea in a particular biblical passage to illustrate the theme. For example we have used the story of the feeding of the 5,000 under the "sharing" theme, although we are very aware that the major significance of this story is the message it conveys about Jesus Christ. However, it also carries the subsidiary theme of "sharing that costs" and can therefore legitimately be used in that context, providing that its main theological theme is also pointed out.

Thirdly we have sometimes made the decision not to use particular biblical material because of the difficulty of the issues it raises. For example we have not included the biblical image of judgement as "everlasting fire" in the theme on fire. The theme of judgement is tackled elsewhere through the story of Noah, the parable of the Sheep and the Goats and under the titles of God.

Inevitably there will be those who will disagree, on either theological or educational grounds, with both our selection and grouping of the texts. We trust they will recognize the complexity of the task we have undertaken in trying to balance the need to present the Bible in a way that respects its integrity and the need to use it in a way that promotes educational goals.

3. The text should stimulate the imagination and extend thought

In rewording the biblical material we have sometimes used storytelling techniques such as flashback and reminiscence as a way of engaging the imagination. In addition there are, in places, imaginative embellishments to the text which we trust serve to make it live for the hearers, whilst still remaining true to the central meaning. Furthermore we have, on occasions, deliberately used difficult words to provide a basis for language extension and to introduce some basic theological vocabulary.

For these reasons it is important that teachers give some introduction before using any part of this book with a class. How much is required will depend on the age and experience of the particular group involved. Background information is provided to enable teachers to set the scene as necessary. When using this the children should be told that it has been written as though a Christian were explaining to another person the significance of the passage in question for Christians.

4. The use of the Bible should respect the educational context

One thing that should be remembered is that although the Bible was originally written to persuade its readers of the truth of its message, it cannot be used in that way in most educational contexts. We therefore recommend that pupils are made aware that this is the book of the Christians, and not necessarily "their" book. It should be pointed out that the claims to truth that are made within it are those of a particular, albeit very significant, religious group. The language used in the classroom should be non–presumptive, making it clear that the pupils are learning about Christian beliefs which they are not necessarily expected to share. There should be freedom to respond in a way that is appropriate for each child. It must of course not be forgotten that one appropriate response may be belief and commitment. It is not the place of the school either to seek or to deny this. By adopting this strategy teachers will be able to remain true to the biblical intentions whilst still fulfilling their educational responsibilities.

Using the material

This book is one of three volumes which are designed to provide a quarry of accessible and easy–to–use biblical material for the busy teacher. It is a book for dipping into rather than for using systematically. Its main purpose is to provide teachers with theologically and educationally valid ways of using biblical material with children. In schools it will provide ideas for an RE–led topic, an RE component for a topic led by another subject, or for separate RE lessons or units of work. In churches it can, with appropriate adaptations, form the basis for a programme of Bible teaching with children. In the three volumes there are over one hundred Bible passages, retold to make them suitable for reading aloud, or for children to read on their own. For ease of use the passages are organized under twenty–four themes which reflect topics commonly appearing on the primary school curriculum. Each theme contains the following components:

1. Understanding the Biblical ideas

This information will give the teacher the basic theological background information needed to understand the biblical ideas which underpin the theme. The passages grouped under a theme will develop and illustrate these ideas.

2. Introducing the passages

These are various practical ideas for introducing the theme and the biblical passages to children.

3. Other useful passages

This is a list of passages which appear elsewhere in the three volumes under other theme headings, but which might also be useful in developing this particular theme.

4. Cross–curricular links

This section demonstrates how the theme can be developed through other subjects on the curriculum, indicating how the use of biblical material can form a valid part of a wider curriculum planning process. Where appropriate, links with National Curriculum subjects are indicated. The attainment targets cited are those in force at the time of writing.

Teachers will also need to refer to the syllabus of religious education used in their school to ensure that the biblical material is introduced in a way which ensures continuity and progression and fulfils statutory requirements.

5. A Christian perspective

These notes outline how each of the passages is generally interpreted by Christians. They contain information for the teacher to draw on when discussing the passages with children.

6. Points of interest

The points of interest contain background information on each of the passages which put them in context and help in understanding their meaning and significance. Again they are for teacher information and are not designed to be read out to children.

7. The passages

Under each theme heading there are four or five passages retold from the Bible which illustrate that theme. Different types of biblical material have been included, such as story, wise sayings, law and poetry, so that children can experience the different genres of literature which appear in the Bible. All the passages can be read aloud to children, although the story material is particularly suitable for use in this way. The material is designed primarily for use with junior aged children, but can be adapted to be used with other age groups.

The three volumes contain a number of extended stories, such as the Joseph saga, which are divided up into episodes. Episodes from one extended story may appear under different theme headings depending on their main emphasis. Teachers wishing to tell the whole of an extended story will find details of where the other episodes appear by referring to the "Other useful passages" section of the theme where a particular episode appears, or on the contents page of the book.

8. Photocopiable activity pages

At the end of each theme you will find a number of photocopiable pupil activity sheets. These are not meant to be used as unsupported worksheets, but are designed as a resource for pupil work which arises out of their study of the biblical passages in that theme. Teachers are also allowed to photocopy the relevant biblical passages from this book if they wish, so that children can refer to the passage whilst using the activity sheet. On the activity sheets children are often referred to the story and asked to read it. With younger junior children it may be necessary to read the story to them.

Two final points

1. Health and safety
As in all teaching, it is essential to ensure that all materials and procedures used in the classroom are safe. For example, glues and paints should be non–toxic and kites should be flown away from power cables with gloves worn whilst holding them. All equipment should undergo regular safety checks. Please consult your school policy document and other relevant Health and Safety regulations.

2. Acts of worship
The passages are short enough to be read in an act of worship. Those grouped together under one theme could be used to create a series of "assemblies".

Activities may need to be added, including the more reflective aspects characteristic of an act of worship — for example prayers, music or a time for thinking about the theme whilst a poem is read.

Notes

1. Francis, Leslie, *Religion In The Primary School* (Collins, 1987)
2. Birnie, Ian, "Is Teaching the Bible too Dangerous a Task for Schools?" in *British Journal of Religious Education,* Vol 5:3, Summer 1983
3. Gower, Ralph, *Religious Education At The Primary Stage* (Lion, 1990)
4. Hull, John, *God–Talk with Young Children* (Christian Education Movement, 1991)
5. Wood, Angela, "Not Whether But How" in *Discernment,* Vol 6, No I, July 1992. Available from CCBI. 35–41, Lower Marsh, London, SEI 7RL
6. *See* Copley, Terence, *About The Bible* (Bible Society, 1990) for further information.
7. Westhill College, *Assessing, Recording and Reporting RE* (Westhill College, Birmingham 1991) p 23

INDEX

Subjects listed in this index span all three volumes of the Resource Bank series. The figure printed in bold indicates the volume number, and the figure which follows is the page reference.

LIVING WISELY

Understanding the biblical ideas

Biblical wisdom is not just intelligence, though it can mean that. Wisdom has a variety of meanings in the Bible. There is a practical wisdom which orders everyday life in a reasonable way. This side of Biblical wisdom would integrate well in the PSE/RE aspect of a topic looking at personal relationships and rules for living. Wisdom can lead to a well–disciplined life and success in various areas. Wisdom can apply to abilities such as needlework and carpentry, military strategy and political administation.

People can be "wise in their own eyes," but not necessarily wise in anybody else's! Wisdom was seen as an attribute of God, and all wisdom, whether profound or mundane, was seen as a gift from him. Wisdom is sometimes personified in the Bible. It is referred to as a wandering female teacher calling out to her disciples.

Wisdom can mean a right relationship with God: "The fear of God is the beginning of wisdom." It is holding God in a rightful awe and thereby getting other things in perspective. Wisdom can be the ability to tell right from wrong in moral matters. It can be the ability to discern what God wants in a certain situation or being able to understand what God is saying.

Wisdom was a gift highly prized. It is described as more precious than jewels. Solomon knew its worth, and chose wisdom before other gifts.

God is described as wise, which is reflected in the beauty and intricacy of creation. Jesus is given the title "wisdom" by Saint Paul. Jesus may have been called this because wisdom is linked to the communicating aspect of God. God reveals himself in nature (creation) and the "wise" can see him there. He reveals himself through special dreams and the "wise" can understand them (Joseph, Daniel). God finally reveals himself in Jesus: that means he shows what he is like through him. He shows what he is like through a man born into poverty with no university education, no power or political influence; a man who died a criminal's death at a young age. The gospel was dubbed as foolishness at the time rather than wisdom.

Introducing the passages

Bring in a number of presents you have been given and discuss gifts with the children. Explore the idea of invisible gifts and introduce the story of Solomon's invisible gift.

Look at some suitable "advice columns" from young people's magazines. Choose these with care. Read the material entitled "Advice from the Preacher".

Discuss the ordinary dreams we all have. Talk about the way special dreams were seen, in the Bible, as carrying a message from God. These were very special dreams, not just any dreams. Look at the dreams Joseph and Daniel interpreted. What was the message contained in them?

Other useful passages

"The Wise Men's Gifts", page 106.

"Understanding the Holy Spirit", Book 3, page 97. Wisdom is seen as one of the gifts the Holy Spirit brings.

The rest of the Daniel story can be found in Book 3, pages 6, 107.

The rest of the Joseph story can be found on pages 67; Book 1, 46–47.

Foolishness is the opposite of wisdom. In Biblical terms foolishness is living life without reference to God. The parable called "The Rich Fool", Book 1, page 63, is an example of this.

"The Two Houses", Book 1, page 99, contrasts wise and foolish builders.

Jesus' teaching could also be included under this title. See particularly "The Sermon on the Mount", pages 19, 20.

Cross–curricular links

English

- Read the story about *The Fourth Wise Man* retold by R H Lloyd (Mowbray, 1984). In what ways were the wise men, wise? What do you think really happened? Make up your own ending to the story. What do you think the expression "To be wise after the event" means? With a group of friends can you dramatize a scenario to show that you understand the expression? Or you could make a script for a radio play and tape it. (1, 2, 3)
- Make a collection of wisdom from the Bible using the book of Proverbs. (2, 3)
- Turn the story of Solomon's invisible gift into a playlet. (EAT 1, 2)

Science

- Christians believe God's wisdom is reflected in creation. Survey the local environment and identify an area where human activity has "spoilt" that creation in some way. Is there any small area around your home, school, church, etc., that you, as part of a group, could try to improve? Be sure that you have good ecological advice. Give an account of your project using writing and photographs. (1, 2) (GAT 5)

Music

- Set the journey of the Three Wise Men to music, as they crossed deserts, cities, an oasis, etc. Use appropriate musical sounds. (1)
- Learn the song "Turn, turn, turn" which is based on Ecclesiastes 3. This can be found in *Alleluya* (A & C Black, 1980) (1)
- The song "Bind us Together" can be found in *Songs and Hymns of Fellowship*. (1)

- Listen to the appropriate part of *Joseph and the Amazing Technicolor Dreamcoat* concerning the butler, the baker and Pharaoh's dreams. (2)

Art

- King Solomon was thought to have been very wise. Jesus said that even King Solomon in all his glory was not as beautiful as the flowers of the fields. Flowers demonstrate the wisdom of God in creation. Look at flower paintings by famous artists such as Van Gogh, Redon, Fantin–Latour and Cezanne on postcards. Cut up a postcard into sections. With a group of friends work together on individual sections to reproduce the original. Concentrate on style, form and colour. (1, 2)

Personal and Social Education

- Discuss societies in which old age and wisdom, which is regarded as accompanying it, are highly respected. In these societies, the elders are the most influential members of the community. Compare this with the way the elderly are valued within Western society. (EAT 1)

Technology

- Wisdom in the Old Testament included metalwork, carpentry, needlecraft, carving, etc. Such skills were seen as God's practical wisdom. Using various wools embroider a wise saying onto canvas. The wisdom should be in the skill that goes into it, as well as the saying. This can be done as a group. (1, 2)

PE/Dance

- Interpret the song "Turn, turn, turn" in dance. (KS 1/2)

SOLOMON'S INVISIBLE GIFT

1 Kings 3 ▶ *page 4*

A Christian perspective

The practical nature of wisdom is illustrated by this story but even such practical wisdom is seen as a gift from God.

Points of interest

1. Children were considered to be a great blessing and very precious. Surrounding nations practised child sacrifice, though how frequent a practice this was is unknown. The Romans abandoned unwanted children.
2. Solomon gambled on the real mother being willing to part with her child rather than to hurt him.

3. The women in this case appeal directly to the king, the supreme judge in the land who exercised God's justice for the people.

ADVICE FROM THE PREACHER

Ecclesiastes 3.1–8,12; 4.9, 10, 12; 5.10; 9.18; 12.12 ▶ *page 5*

A Christian perspective

The main point of the poem is that there is an appropriate time for different aspects of life, though the writer could just be describing the different facets of life without making judgements. War, hatred, love, birth— these things happen.

Birth and death, laughter and tears, hurt and healing are parts of life. They are two sides of a coin and cannot be avoided. Our imperfect world without tears would be wrong. It is right to cry over some things.

Points of interest

There are three difficult phrases: "a time to hate", "a time for war", and "a time to kill". The latter I have translated "hurt". You can use these as a basis for discussion. Is there a time when war is appropriate, though something to grieve over? Is there ever a time to kill (not "murder")?

Teacher resource

The chorus of the song "Bind us together, Lord", by Bob Gillman, referred to on the worksheet on page 12, is as follows:

Bind us together, Lord,
Bind us together with cords that cannot be broken.
Bind us together, Lord,
Bind us together,
Bind us together with love.

Copyright © 1977 Thankyou Music,
P.O. Box 75, Eastbourne, East Sussex,
BN23 6NW, UK. Used by permission.

JOSEPH AND PHARAOH'S DREAMS

JOSEPH: EPISODE 2
Genesis 37.36; 39.1–41, 57 ▶ *page 6*

A Christian perspective

During his time in Egypt, Joseph's fortunes changed. He went from being slave to Prime Minister. The writer emphasizes God making provision for the future. Joseph was in the right place at the right time. He not only saved his own family but Egypt as well. Dreams were seen as significant, and there was a class of wise men skilled at interpreting them. Joseph (like Daniel) does not claim to be one of these, only to have wisdom from God.

Points of interest

1. The prison system of Egypt was very well organized. Each prisoner's records were entered under seven different headings!

2. Egypt was the breadbasket of the ancient world, but, like most countries of the Middle East, suffered periodic famines. The regular floods of the Nile kept the land fertile, but, apart from the Nile, the land is very dry. If the floods fail, famine ensues.

3. The cupbearer was the butler. He tasted the wine to make sure it was not poisoned.

DANIEL AND THE KING'S DREAMS

DANIEL: EPISODE 1
Daniel 2 ▶ *page 8*

A Christian perspective

In this story Daniel is seen as possessing great wisdom because it had been given to him by God. Wisdom is one of the characteristics of God in the Bible, it is also a gift which can be given to humans. In this case it is supernatural wisdom rather than practical wisdom for life.

The actual dream was of a statue with a head of gold, a chest of silver, hips of bronze, legs of iron and feet of clay (mixed or coated with iron). A large stone smashes the statue at its weakest point, the feet of clay. The statue represents the great empires of the world, such as Nebuchadnezzar's, which will one day fall.

Points of interest

1. Great store was set by dreams in the ancient world. That did not mean that just any dream was important. Some dreams were seen as special, such as Pharaoh's dreams which Joseph interpreted.

2. Nebuchadnezzar was the ruler of the Babylonian Empire, its last really great king. Like most Middle Eastern leaders, he had a group of wise men. Daniel is different to the other wise men as his wisdom comes from Israel's God. Nebuchadnezzar's threat is quite plausible. Darius I ordered the wholesale murder of his wise men.

Solomon's Invisible Gift

1 Kings 3

Solomon looked down from his throne at the two women in front of him. They both seemed very upset. He wondered what problem they were bringing to him to solve. He nodded to them to begin.

At once one of them started to explain. "My Lord, this woman and I share a house. A few days ago I had a baby boy. Then three days later, this woman had a son too. As soon as I woke up this morning, I picked up my baby to feed him. He was dead! I couldn't believe it! I began to examine him to see what was wrong. Then I realized he wasn't my baby! This other woman had got my baby! Her son must have died in the night and while I was asleep she swapped them over."

"She's lying!" the other woman shouted. "My son is alive! Hers is dead!"

"I'm not lying!" the first woman shouted back. "My son is alive!"

The king listened to them arguing. He looked at the baby. What a decision to have to make! How glad he was that he did not have to make it alone. For Solomon had had a strange dream soon after becoming king. God had asked him to choose any gift he wanted for himself. Solomon had not asked for wealth, for long life or for success in battle. He'd asked for wisdom, so that he would know what was the right thing to do. "I am only young," he'd said, "and I do not know enough to be a good king. If I am going to rule over all your chosen people fairly and make them happy, then I shall need great wisdom."

Now, as everyone waited for his decision, Solomon remembered God's promise to give him this gift. He said, "Each woman says that this child is hers. Bring me a sword." Then he ordered, "Cut the child in two and give them half each." He held his breath. Would it work? What would he do if they called his bluff? He certainly wouldn't harm the child!

Immediately the first woman shouted, "Oh no! Don't do that! Give him to her! He belongs to her!"

Everyone looked at Solomon. What would he do? Solomon himself knew what to do now. "The first woman is the boy's real mother. Give her the baby," he said — because he knew that only the real mother would choose to give away her son rather than see him killed. Now, the baby's mother took her baby and cuddled him. She was glad to have him back! As they watched her leave, the people realized just how wise the king had been.

Examples of Solomon's wisdom:
Solomon collected wise sayings. Here are some from the book of Proverbs:

A gentle answer calms down anger but a bitter one stirs it up. 15.1
The criticism of a friend is better than the flattery of an enemy. 27.6
Sensible people see trouble coming and get out of the way. Stupid people walk straight into it. 27.12

RESOURCE BANK 2: LIVING WISELY

Advice from the Preacher

Ecclesiastes 3.1–8,12; 4.9, 10, 12; 5.10; 9.18; 12.12

The book of Ecclesiastes is a collection of wise sayings from "The Preacher". This is a well–known poem from this book.

There is a time for everything,
A time for every part of life.
A time to be born and a time to die,
A time to plant and a time to pull up,
A time to hurt and a time to heal,
A time to pull down and a time to rebuild,
A time to cry and a time to laugh,
A time to be sad and a time to dance with joy,
A time to look for things and a time to give in,
A time to keep hold of things and a time to let go,
A time to destroy and a time to mend,
A time to be silent and a time to speak,
A time to hate and a time to love,
A time for war and a time for peace.
(Ecclesiastes 3.1–8)

Other wisdom from the preacher:

Of the making of books there is no end, and too much study wears you out. (Ecclesiastes 12.12)

I know that there is nothing better for people than to be happy and to do good while they live. (Ecclesiastes 3.12)

Two are better than one. If one person falls down a friend can help that person!
   One person may be overpowered, two can defend each other, but a cord made of three strands cannot easily be broken. (Ecclesiastes 4.9, 10, 12)

Whoever loves money, never has money enough. (Ecclesiastes 5.10)

Wisdom is better than the weapons of war. (Ecclesiastes 9.18)

Joseph and Pharaoh's Dreams

JOSEPH: EPISODE 2

Genesis 37.36; 39.1–41, 57

Pharaoh's cupbearer hurried over to Joseph. "Pharaoh has sent for me," he told him, "just as you said he would three days ago. I hope you were right about the rest of my dream too."

"Yes, I was right," Joseph told him. "God told me what your dream meant. Now remember, after Pharaoh has forgiven you and given you your old job back, remember to tell him about me. Tell him I've done nothing wrong and that I don't deserve to be in here."

"Yes, yes, I'll remember," the man said impatiently as he hurried from the prison cell. The doors closed behind him.

Joseph leaned back on the rough wall. How long it seemed since he had first arrived in Egypt, and had been sold as a slave to Potiphar, Pharaoh's captain of the guard. He thought back to his time in Potiphar's house. With God's help, he had done all his duties there so well that soon Potiphar had trusted him to run the whole household for him. For a time, Joseph had been happy in a way. He had come to believe that God had a reason for everything that happened — even though Joseph did not understand it.

But then, Potiphar's wife had falsely accused Joseph of attacking her. She lied about Joseph to her husband, and Potiphar had thrown him into prison. Even here, with God's help, Joseph had done well, and the warder trusted him to help with his work. Here, Joseph had met the man who had worked as Pharaoh's cupbearer until he had displeased Pharaoh and had been thrown into prison. When this man had dreamed a strange dream, God had helped Joseph to tell him what it meant.

"And now — at this moment — he might be telling Pharaoh all about me!" Joseph thought excitedly. "I might be free by tomorrow!"

But tomorrow came and went, and the next day, and the next. In the end, Joseph had to admit to himself that the man had forgotten all about his friend in prison, in his excitement at being back in Pharaoh's favour.

So two whole years passed, and Joseph was still a prisoner. But then, one morning, Pharaoh got out of bed in a terrible mood. He sent for all his wise men and advisers. "Tell me what my dreams meant last night!" he ordered. "Listen!

"I dreamed I was standing near the River Nile. Suddenly, out of the river came seven cows! They were fat and healthy looking, and they settled down to graze on the bank. Then seven other cows appeared! These were not like the first seven: they were thin and obviously starving. They went over to the fat cows — and ate them! But they didn't grow a bit fatter!

"Then I had a second dream. This time, I counted seven ears of corn — fat and healthy — growing on a single stalk. While I watched, seven other ears grew on the stem, but these were thin and withered, scorched by the hot wind. These

RESOURCE BANK 2: LIVING WISELY

swallowed up the seven healthy ears. Now tell me what these two dreams mean."

Pharaoh's advisers were horrified. They had no idea of the meaning. But then his cupbearer, listening to all this, suddenly remembered Joseph.

"Pharaoh," he said, "you have reminded me of a promise I have broken. While I was in prison, there was a young man there, a Hebrew slave. He was able to explain dreams. I promised him that I would tell you about him, but I forgot."

So Pharaoh sent for Joseph who hurriedly tidied himself up. "I've been told you can explain the meaning of dreams," Pharaoh said to him.

"No I can't," Joseph said — to the cupbearer's horror! "But God can, and he will help me." Then Joseph listened to Pharaoh's account of his dreams.

"These two dreams mean the same thing," he said. "Listen. The great River Nile makes the land of Egypt fertile. So for the next seven years your harvests, watered by the river's flood, will be heavy and rich — just as you watched the seven fat cows come out of the Nile. But then the floods will fail. No rain will fall for seven long years, the crops will die, and your people will starve. It will be as if the seven good years had not happened.

"So now you must find a wise and reliable man, and put him in charge of all the harvests in Egypt. He and his officials must take a fifth of each year's harvest for the next seven years. All this food must be stored in great barns in each city. Then, when the famine comes, this man must supervise the distribution of the stored food so that your people will survive."

Pharaoh realized how good this plan was. "I do not think I will find anyone else as well suited to this job as Joseph himself," he said. "For he has his God to help him."

From that moment, Joseph's life changed dramatically. He became rich and powerful, second only to Pharaoh himself. During the next seven years, Joseph travelled throughout Egypt, organizing the building of the great barns, and watching as they filled with grain from the rich harvests.

When the famine began, Joseph opened these barns: his officials gave out fair shares of the wheat to all, and the Egyptians had enough to eat. As the famine spread, people from other countries also ran out of food. Among them was Joseph's own family, back home in Canaan.

Daniel and the King's Dream

DANIEL: EPISODE 1

Daniel 2

Daniel hurried to his house to tell his friends what they must do. Since they had been captured in Israel and brought to live here in Babylon, in the king's palace, they had served the king well and pleased him by the widsom and knowledge they had shown. But now they were all in danger — Daniel and his three friends, Shadrach, Meshach and Abednego, as well as all King Nebuchadnezzar's other advisers. For the king had set them an impossible task and said he would kill them if they couldn't do it!

Daniel explained what had happened. "Nebuchadnezzar told some of his wisest officials that he had had a strange dream and wanted to know what it meant. He wouldn't even tell them what the dream was: they have to describe it to him as well and explain its meaning! It's impossible, of course, for any of us to do that. But if someone doesn't explain it to him, we will all be killed! When I heard about it, I asked the king to give me some time to think. We must ask God to describe the dream to us, and to explain what it means. Only God can save us."

So Daniel and his three friends began to pray, and, during the night, God showed Daniel what he needed to know. Then Daniel thanked God for saving them:

"Praise God for ever!
He is the source of all wisdom and strength.
He is greater than all human kings.
He is a God who changes history.
He gives wisdom to the wise,
and knowledge to those who seek understanding.
I thank you God that you have given me wisdom and strength.
Thank you for telling me the king's dream."

When Daniel had finished praying, he hurried to the king.

"Can you tell me what I saw in my dream and explain it?" Nebuchadnezzar asked eagerly when he saw Daniel.

"No!" replied Daniel. "No man can know such secrets. Only God can tell you what you dreamed, and what it all means and he has told me. Listen...."

Then Daniel described Nebuchadnezzar's dream just as he had dreamed it. Then he went on to explain it all to him. The king was amazed. "Your God must indeed be the real God !" he said, and he appointed Daniel as ruler over Babylon, and promoted his three friends too.

RESOURCE BANK 2: LIVING WISELY

Wisdom Personified

Sometimes ideas are referred to as people. This is called "personification". This is a long word: it just means turning an idea, or a thing into a person.

If the word "wisdom" were to become a person, what sort of person would it be?

Activity

• Write about wisdom as a person.

• What would a person called "Wisdom" look like? How would they behave? What would they say?

Think about it

The Bible writes about wisdom as a teacher, a female teacher, who calls to people to listen to her. What do you think she might be saying? Can you think of one thing she might say to people today?

Read some of Solomon's wise sayings on page 4.
Read Proverbs 8.1–11. What is "wisdom" saying in this passage?

The Queen of Sheba

The Bible tells the story of the visit of the Queen of Sheba. She had heard how wise Solomon was, so she decided to visit him to find out for herself. You can read this story in 1 Kings 10.1–13.

Activity

• This riddle is known as the Queen of Sheba's riddle. It is not found in the Bible though the Bible says she tested his wisdom with riddles and difficult questions. Can you solve the Queen of Sheba's riddle?

"When I am alive I do not move. When I have my head cut off I move. What am I?"

- There is another riddle in the Bible – you can find it in Judges 14.14.

  Out of the eater came something to eat;
  Out of the strong came something sweet.

  Can you solve this riddle too? You will find a clue on a tin of Tate and Lyle's Golden Syrup: they use this riddle as a trade mark.

- It was not only Solomon's ability to answer riddles that impressed the Queen of Sheba, but his general widsom . Read the story called "Solomon's Invisible Gift" on page 4. How does this story show his wisdom?

  Answers to riddles: The answer to Sheba's riddle is "A Tree". When a tree is alive it stands still in the earth. Cut down, it makes the mast for a ship and moves. The answer to Samson's riddle is — "bees making honey in a dead lion".

The Threefold Cord

You will find this piece of wisdom on page 5 called "Advice from the Preacher".

Activity

• Can you devise a safe and fair way of testing this? Are three strands really stronger than one?

Think about it

The writer of this piece of wisdom was talking about friendship. Think about what he said. Have there been times when having friends has been a strength to you?

The song "Bind us together, Lord" (page 3) expresses similar ideas to the saying about the threefold cord. You might like to play it, learn to sing it or listen to others singing it.

A Time for Everything

Read this passage on page 5 called "Advice from the Preacher".

In this poem the "Preacher" is describing all the different things which happen in life.

Group activity

- Practise reading this poem. It can be read in several ways:

  As a group — this involves the whole group reading the poem together.

  One line at a time — for this each person says a line in turn.

  Antiphonal speaking — split the group in two. The two groups face each other. Group one speaks one line, group two the next and so on.

  Cumulative speaking — for this, one person speaks the first line, two people speak the second line, three the third, etc.

LAWS FOR LIVING

Understanding the biblical ideas

The word used most often of Law in the Old Testament is Torah, a word that indicates teaching, direction and guidance. Law is a way of life, not just a list of dos and don'ts. It is described as more precious than gold and sweeter than honey. It is seen as a gift from God, not a burden.

Law gives the freedom to live in peace and trust. The penalties attached to Law are there to help correct the negative tendencies in humanity, to stop people wrecking their own and others' lives.

Social justice is expressed through the Law, which particularly protects the poor and powerless: the orphan, the stranger, and the widow.

The Law is to be obeyed from the heart. External compliance was never enough. Breaking the Law is not breaking a list of rules: it is breaking a relationship, hurting God and others.

God chose Israel before he gave them the Law. The only reason for God's choice is love. The Law, however, regulates the relationship. The Law is then kept as a result of that relationship.

The old Law is not abandoned. Jesus told his followers they must outdo the Pharisees in keeping the Law. The laws of the Old Testament are fulfilled in the law of Jesus. There is a tension in the Old Testament for it proclaimed both "An eye for an eye", and forgiveness — even of the enemy. The New Testament pushes the Old Testament ideal of forgiveness to its limits, making "Love your enemies" the norm.

Unjust laws are an insult to God. Laws should reflect the character of God. God is holy, just and loving: human law should be the same.

God is described as a just judge who enforces the Law and who refuses to let injustice and evil go unchecked.

Introducing the passages

Explore rules of the road, school and home. Discuss the various functions of rules. Look at laws of the land and their function.

Rules are for living together in harmony and for protection. They mark out what is acceptable behaviour and what isn't. Talk about making the rules. Who decides the rules at home, at school, in the state? How are rules changed?

Who decided the rules of the Bible? Look at the Ten Commandments and how they are worked out in detailed laws. You will need the passages entitled "Old Testament and New Testament Laws," and "The Ten Commandments" for this. Read the Sermon on the Mount, and discuss how radically this would change people's way of life.

Discuss losing precious things and introduce the story of Josiah.

Other useful passages

"Advice from the Bible on Sharing", Book 1, pages 68–69. This includes some of the laws on sharing.

"The Rich Fool", Book 1, page 63. Laws on sharing are broken in this story. "Three Friends in the Fire", page 78. This is an example of a law kept.

"Naboth's Vineyard", page 33. This is an example of a law broken.

"Creation Spoilt", page 93. Another example of a law broken.

"The Good Samaritan", Book 3, page 19. This shows the outworking of the Law.

The rest of the Moses story can be found in Book 1, pages 19–20, 23; Book 2, 21, 49–50, 77, 81; Book 3, 82.

Cross–curricular links

English
- Where do you meet rules and regulations? Make a list of rules at home, at school, in the street. Do you think they are all good or helpful? Could you write your own rules for school, the classroom or the home? You will need to think of the needs of others as well as yourself. (3)
- Spelling also has rules: investigate some common word patterns, letter strings, word families and their relationships. (4)

Personal and Social Education
- Look at laws concerning drinking and smoking and the reason for those laws. Look at posters about drink–driving — why is it necessary? Why aren't people more responsible? (EAT 1, 2)
- Look at unfair laws in terms of gender and race. Why is legislation sometimes needed in these areas? (EAT 1, 2)

Science
- Look at rules to live by for keeping healthy: a balanced diet, oral hygiene, avoidance of harmful substances. (2)

Technology
- Design and make your own set of road signs: which shape and colour would you use to denote warning? Electrical circuits can be incorporated to make them light up. Design a poster to persuade people not to smoke or not to drink and drive. (1, 2) (SAT 4)

Mathematics
- Look at the four rules. Explore the relationship between them. (1, 2, 3)
- Plan an investigation: limit it to given numbers and operations. Expand as appropriate to the experience and age of the children. Any investigations which have limits or rules could be used. (1, 2, 3)

Geography
- Geography has its own conventions which are universally accepted. Maps have agreed rules, e.g. for reference, coordinates are always read horizontally before vertically. Draw your own map of an island using a grid for ten coordinates (use letters and numbers). (1) (MAT 3)

History
- Use references to research law–making through the ages — the feudal system, Magna Carta, the Poor Laws, etc. Research one in depth. (1, 2, 3) (EAT 2, 3)

Art
- Use calligraphy to write out some of the biblical laws. Investigate various types of script before you choose the one you want to use. (1, 2)
- Find out if a local church has the Ten Commandments engraved in stone or written on the walls. Make a large rubbing if possible. (1) (EAT 4/5)

PE/Dance
- Most games have rules. Why? Can you imagine a game of football without rules. Sometimes rules change to improve a sport, e.g. offside laws. Can you make up a game to play and the rules needed to play it? Try it out together. (KS 2)

Music
- Learn and add your own percussion to "The Beatitudes Song" (Worship Time Songs) and "This Little Light of Mine" (*Alleluya,* A&C Black) both of which are from the Sermon on the Mount. (1) The address for Worship Time Songs (Volume One) is: Worship Time Music, M Grimmitt, 7 Lindsworth Road, Kings Norton, Birmingham, B30 3NH

JOSIAH AND THE LOST SCROLL
2 Chronicles 34 ▶ *page 18*

A Christian perspective
The main point of this story is that the finding of the book of the Law brought about change — at least in some people. The Bible describes the Law as a complete way of life. When the people promised to keep the Law they were pledging themselves to a total change of behaviour, not just the keeping of a few extra laws.

Points of interest
1. The book of the Law is generally assumed to have been Deuteronomy.

2. Josiah was a rebel. His ancestors had been very bad kings and he rebelled against this and started a reform. It began with himself, then moved outwards in wider circles. Although people promised to keep the newly–found Law, not everyone meant it. After Josiah's death, many of them lapsed back into the old ways.

3. In a land in which not everyone one could read, regular public reading of the Law was vital. The people could hardly be blamed if they did not know the Law— the responsibility rested with the king and the priests.

THE SERMON ON THE MOUNT 1
Matthew 5–7; Luke 6.20–49 ▶ *page 19*

A Christian perspective
The word happiness used here is not a superficial feeling. It means "to be congratulated". Christians believe happiness is more than a mental state, it is an attitude towards life. In no way are Christians encouraged to enjoy persecution, grief and ill–treatment. Neither is it resignation. It is happiness in the midst of a life of hardship, and hope in the midst of trouble. The way of life advocated in the Sermon on the Mount is not "pie in the sky when you die". It is a radical reversal of the normal way of life. It is a way of life marked out by a deep relationship with God which may bring persecution but is considered worth it. Heaven is characterized first and foremost by a relationship: it is a relationship which starts on earth and deepens and extends in heaven. It is "pie now and later".

Points of interest
1. The word "poor" was used of people who remained faithful to God under difficult circumstances.
2. Peacemakers are people who actively overcome evil with good.
3. The Sermon on the Mount is not literally a "sermon": it is a collection of teachings given by Jesus.

THE SERMON ON THE MOUNT 2
Matthew 5—7 ▶ *page 20*

A Christian perspective
For Christians, the Sermon on the Mount is not just about good behaviour. It is a radical redrawing of relationships. It is a description of life in the Kingdom, or family, of God. In the salt and light passages, Jesus is calling his followers to make a difference to the world: to shine as an example and to preserve the world from going bad.

Points of interest
1. Salt gathered from the Dead Sea is salt mixed with other chemicals. When the salt is collected, other particles are gathered with it, so it is not pure salt. Jesus here is talking of becoming like the tasteless residue of salt. In a hot country, salt was very important for preservation of food.
2. Light was a precious commodity. Windows in houses were small and high up to keep out the heat. The only light was from a small oil lamp, which gave very little light. Life was generally lived outdoors. What light there was, was highly valued. To put a barrel over it would have been unthinkable. The bowl referred to was probably a Roman measure: it contained about nine litres and it was large enough to cover a lamp.
3. The saying about the speck and plank does not mean people were not allowed to criticize. The saying is about fault finding: it is about having a condemnatory attitude, which is often associated with a blindness to one's own faults.

THE TEN COMMANDMENTS
MOSES: EPISODE 6
Exodus 19—20.17 ▶ *page 21*

A Christian perspective
The Bible sees Law as a gift from a good God to help people live in friendship with him and each other. The cloud and the fire on the mountain top are a symbol of the presence of God. The Ten Commandments are the most important laws. They are the policy statement, the other laws are the out–working of that statement.

The Ten Commandments:
1. The Israelites were to worship only one God. The relationship with God is like an exclusive marriage relationship.
2. Images were not allowed. When God spoke to Israel from the Mountain of Sinai, there was no form, only a voice.
3. God's name was not to be used inappropriately or in rites involving magic.
4. The Sabbath rest reflects not only God's rest after creation, but the rest of the slaves after liberation.
5. Parents are honoured as the givers of life.
6. The word used is murder, not kill. The Israelites fought in the army so they did kill in battle but murder was forbidden.
7. The family was sacred and not to be broken by adultery. A woman was also a man's property.
8. Stealing could lead to death in a poor country when theft of an animal, or of what little wealth a family had, could mean starvation.
9. Perjury was forbidden because it caused untold harm and insulted a God of truth. A person bearing false witness was supposed to suffer the same penalty as the victim would have suffered if found guilty as a result of perjury.
10. Envy could easily lead to stealing. This law dealt with motive and thoughts.

Points of interest
1. The name represents the person, therefore God's name was to be treated respectfully.

2. The biblical writers were careful over their use of language when describing God, though God's hands, eyes and face are referred to poetically. Sculpture as an art form was not really developed in Israel because of this ban on images.

NEW TESTAMENT AND OLD TESTAMENT LAWS
John 13.34–35; Luke 6.31; Matthew 7.12; 22.34–40; Deuteronomy 10.19; 14.22, 15.12–14; 16.18–19; 19.15; 22.8; 24.14, 15, 17; 25.15 ▶ *page 22*

A Christian perspective

The Bible does not present the Law as a list of dos and don'ts, it is a complete way of life, lived in friendship with God. The laws regulate that friendship. There are many different words for Law in the Old Testament — one is Torah. The very word Torah indicates direction. The Law indicates a way or direction for life. The Ten Commandments were the great principles, the "policy statement". The other laws are those great principles applied to daily life.

"Thou shalt not steal," is applied as: "Make sure your weights and measures are accurate and pay promptly." The poor had no resources, so cheating them with false weights or not paying them promptly caused great hardship.

"Thou shalt not murder," is worked out in the various cases of manslaughter, and included making the house safe so that people were not killed accidentally.

The tithe reflected the Christian belief that everything belongs to God: giving one tenth was an acknowledgement of this.

There are several principles at work in the Law:
• Copy God. God is just, and good human laws should reflect that.
• Look at what God has done for you. "You were strangers in Egypt, therefore look after the stranger."
• Humanitarian concern. Protect the defenceless: "the widow, the orphan and the stranger."

Points of interest

1. Jesus said that the summary of the Law covers all of the Ten Commandments. Law either relates to God or to others.
2. "The Golden Rule" was known in Judaism, in the negative form. "Do not do unto others what you wouldn't want them to do to you."
3. Jesus told his disciples to copy his love. This echoes the command to the Israelites to copy God.

Josiah and the Lost Scroll

2 Chronicles 34

The work in the Temple was under way. All day the carpenters and the stonemasons were busy. The king had sent them all the money given by the people to pay for the repairs. Supplies of wood and of stone were arriving, and, slowly, God's Temple was beginning to look beautiful again, after the years of neglect.

King Josiah was pleased to hear about the work. He had been king now for eighteen years — since he was eight, in fact! He wanted to serve God and to please him, but it was difficult because he couldn't be sure what God wanted him to do. Even the priest could not tell him all he needed to know. Josiah's father and grandfather, the last two kings, had not tried to follow God. They had done many wrong things. But Josiah was sure about one thing: God would want his Temple to be made beautiful again.

The secretary came in, disturbing Josiah's thoughts. He gave a brief report on the work in the Temple, and then he said, "Hilkiah the priest has given me a scroll for you. He found it in the Temple where the men are working. He thought you would be interested in it: listen." And he began to read from it.

Josiah listened for a few minutes — and then interrupted excitedly. "It's the book of the Law!" he cried. "It tells us exactly what God wants us to do! At last we've found it. Go on!"

But, as the secretary read on, Josiah became more and more upset. He and his people had done so many wrong things because they had not known how God wanted them to live! What could he do? He must act at once.

He called all the people together to the Temple. There, he read out all of the Laws to the people. Together Josiah and his people made a fresh start. They promised to keep God's laws in future and to live as God wanted them to.

The Sermon on the Mount 1

Matthew 5—7; Luke 6.20–49

Jesus sat down on the hillside above the crowds, so that they could all see and hear him easily. Then he began to teach them.

"Happy are the people who know they need God's help, for they are his followers and will live with him for ever.

   "Happy are the people who are grieving or sorrowful, for God himself will comfort them.

   "Happy are the people who do not think too highly of themselves and who are not proud. They will reign with God.

   "Happy are those people who wish only to do what God wants them to do. He will give them everything they need.

   "Happy are the people who care for each other, and forgive each other. God will care for them and forgive them.

   "Happy are the people who only think about what is good, and have nothing to do with evil things. They will be able to be with God himself.

   "Happy are the people who bring peace to others instead of hatred and fighting. They will be called 'sons and daughters of God'.

   "Happy are those who suffer cruelty because they believe in God, and because they stand up for what is right. They will be part of God's great Kingdom.

Don't be sad when people insult you or treat you cruelly or tell lies about you, just because you believe in me and follow me. Even while you suffer these things, remember this: that God has already prepared a great reward for you to receive in heaven. So be glad, deep down, because of this. Remember, people have always treated God's followers badly."

The Sermon on the Mount 2

Matthew 5—7

Salt and Light

If you follow me you are like salt for the earth. Salt preserves the goodness of food for us. It gives our meals flavour, and helps us to enjoy them. So you, as my followers, should preserve and look after what is good in the world. It should be good for other people to have you among them, bringing them a taste of my own love and care for them. Think: if salt itself loses saltiness, it becomes useless — then it is of no help at all. It is just thrown out with the other rubbish. So make sure you keep your "saltiness" — your "flavour" of goodness.

In the same way, my followers should be like light for the rest of the world. Light gives life and health to us, and it guides us. So you should be like that to other people, showing them what is good, helping them to do the right things by your example, and bringing only good to them. If a person lights a lamp, they don't hide it under a bowl. No, they put it high up, on a stand or a shelf, so that it lights the whole house. In the same way, you must not hide your "light" — your knowledge of God and of his love. So, people will see how you live, and will realize that your goodness comes from God's love for you. Then they, too, will praise God.

Speck and Plank

One person judging another is like someone saying to their friend, "Let me take that speck of sawdust from your eye," when they have a great plank sticking out of their own. Do not be quick to find fault with others. Just think about all the faults in your own life, and concentrate on getting rid of those.

The Ten Commandments

MOSES: EPISODE 6

Exodus 19—20.17

They were glad to stop. They had been moving steadily southwards since they had left Egypt. Now they had arrived at Mount Sinai: here they rested.

They looked up at the mountain. Moses and Aaron were up there somewhere, for Moses was talking to God. Great clouds of smoke billowed about the mountain, and rose into the air. Within the cloud, the Israelites could see flashes of fire. They were frightened as they slowly realized how great and powerful God must be. That morning Moses and Aaron had gone up the mountain. Moses would talk to God, and then pass on God's message to the people.

At last Moses and Aaron returned to them. Moses brought them the special teaching which God wanted his people to hear. The people were eager to learn God's directions for their lives.

"God said you are his special people," said Moses. "You belong to him and he is your God. He has given you these laws so that you might live in friendship with God and each other. You must obey God' s laws and live as he wants you to. God has promised to be with us always and to lead us to our new land. These are the laws he has given:

'I am the Lord your God. I rescued you from slavery in Egypt.

'You must worship only me.

'You must not make a statue of anyone or anything nor worship such a statue.

'You must use my name with respect to show that you honour me.

'Remember that the Sabbath day is my special day. You must not do any work on it.

'Treat your parents with love and respect.

'You must not murder anyone.

'You must not take anybody else's wife or husband.

'You must not take anything that does not belong to you.

'Never tell lies about other people.

'Do not be jealous of anyone's belongings. Do not wish that you had them.'"

New Testament and Old Testament Laws

The Ten Commandments were the most important laws that God gave to the Israelites. But he also gave them many others, to help them to live together in their new land in peace, prosperity and happiness. Here are just a few of them. You can find the Old Testament laws on sharing in Book 1, page 68.

Look after the strangers in your land, just as God looked after you when you were strangers in Egypt. (Deuteronomy 10.19)

Treat orphans and strangers and widows as you would anyone else. Do not cheat them just because they have no one to defend them. (Deuteronomy 24.17)

Set aside one tenth of your harvest each year as a thank you to God. (Deuteronomy 14.22)

If one of your own people has worked as your slave for six years, then let him go free, if he wishes, in the seventh year, with enough animals and seed for him to support himself in the future. (Deuteronomy 15.12–14)

Appoint people as judges. But make sure that all of you act justly and fairly all the time. Do not give or accept bribes to alter decisions. (Deuteronomy 16.18–19)

Never find a person guilty on the evidence of just one witness. There must be two or three witnesses of the crime. (Deuteronomy 19.15)

If a person builds themselves a new house, they should make sure they build a strong wall around the edge of the roof, so no one can fall off it. (Deuteronomy 22.8)

If someone does some work for you, make sure they are paid promptly. (Deuteronomy 24.14–15)

Make sure that all weighing and measuring is accurate when you buy and sell things. (Deuteronomy 25.15)

The New Testament
Jesus once said that the two most important laws out of the many in the Old Testament were these two:

Love the Lord your God with all your heart, and with all your soul, and with all your mind, and love and care for your neighbour as you love and care for yourself. (Matthew 22.34–40) (Deuteronomy 6.5; Leviticus 19.18)

Before he died, Jesus gave his followers a new law or commandment: "A new law I give you, that you love one another even as I have loved you. By this love, people should know you are my followers." (John 13.34–35)

This law has been called "The Golden Rule".

Do to other people what you would want them to do to you. (Matthew 7.12; Luke 6.31)

RESOURCE BANK 2: LAWS FOR LIVING

Behind Bars

Shakespeare, a famous play writer, called jealousy a "green–eyed monster".
What sort of monsters would these words make?

Selfishness, Envy, Hatred, Lies

Lie Monster.

Activity

- Choose one of the words above.

- Think about the sort of monster your word would be if it turned into a monster.
  In drama, create a short sketch with a friend showing how your monster would
  behave. If you prefer, you can write about how your monster would behave.

Think about it

A good law acts like a cage. Just as a cage might stop a monster causing harm,
so a law can stop "monstrous behaviour" causing harm.

Take a sheet of paper and draw a monster on it.

Now make a series of bars from coloured paper to create a cage. Glue them over your monster.

On the bars write the laws that stop monstrous behaviour. You will find some laws on pages 21 and 22.

Calligrams

Read pages 19 and 20 on "The Sermon on the Mount".

A calligram is a word that is drawn in a way that expresses its meaning.

Example: light might be drawn like this.

Activity

• Choose one word from the list below. Read the teaching from which it is taken (Salt and Light, page 20; Treasure, Book 1, page 68; Love, Book 1, page 83). Decide how you would draw the word to express its meaning.

Love, Treasure, Salt, Light

The Beatitudes

Read the Beatitudes on page 19.

The Maltese Cross has eight arms.
It is the symbol used by the Saint John Ambulance Brigade.

 Group activity

- Make a Maltese Cross. Carefully glue just the edges of each arm to a paper background.

- Each point of this cross stands for one of "the Beatitudes". You will find these on page 19.

- Number the eight arms. Cut eight pieces of paper small enough to slip under each arm. On each piece of paper write one of the Beatitudes. Alternatively design your own way of attaching the eight Beatitudes to the arms of the Maltese Cross.

The Golden Key

Read page 22.

Activity

• Make a key out of gold paper or card.

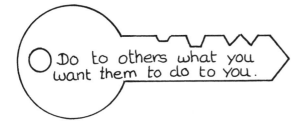

• On one side write Jesus' golden rule.

• On the other, write the two laws which Jesus said summed up all of the Law.

Read the Ten Commandments. You will find these on page 21.

Think about it

Would the two passages on your golden key really sum up all the Law and be the "key" to good behaviour?

OPPOSITES

Understanding the biblical ideas

The Bible presents good and evil as opposing but unequal powers. Christians believe good is stronger than evil and love is stronger than hatred, and the ultimate triumph of good is not in doubt.

Wrong, or sin, is not just doing wrong actions, though it includes that. There are specific sins such as stealing and lying. There is also wrong that is defined by a relationship and by the character of God.

Christians see God as creator, parent and king: someone who is in relationship with humanity in a variety of ways. Wrong is just as much a failure to live in this relationship as it is specific sins. Sin is also seen as rebellion, such as a child rejecting their parents: the wrong lies not only in specific wrongs the child may have done, but in the rejection itself. The story of the prodigal son ("The Son who Left Home" Book 1, page 80) is an example of this type of wrong.

Right and wrong in the Bible are defined by the character of God. God's character is described as holy, just, true, good, and loving. Human behaviour should reflect that. Evil is the opposite of all those things.

Wrong is described in many terms. It is like a debt. Doing wrong puts you in debit. Wrong is also "falling short", "missing the mark": a failure to be all that people were created to be.

The stories in this section offer a variety of contrasts, such as the greed of Ahab in Naboth's vineyard which can be contrasted with the generosity of the widow who gave her last two coins, page 105. There are many other stories which could be used. Teachers could put together pairs of stories to illustrate this theme.

Children can be encouraged to assess the behaviour of characters, asking whether the characters in the stories are living to their full God–given potential and living in friendship with God. Teachers may wish to select a different group of stories which express opposites in reactions, feelings and experiences: stories which demonstrate sorrow and joy, life and death, acceptance and rejection. A list of these stories is also included.

Introducing the passages

Talk with the children about right and wrong and how people decide what is right and what is wrong. Give them situations in which they have to decide on the "right" course of action. Make sure these situations are not too simplistic so that they understand that sometimes decisions are difficult to make.

Discuss Christian beliefs about right and wrong, as outlined above. You could use a dartboard (using velcro darts) to illustrate falling short of the mark. Look at stories involving contrasts in good and bad behaviour such as "Naboth's Vineyard" and "The Widow's Gift," and "The Death of John the Baptist" and "Paul's Hymn of Love".

Discuss opposites in feelings and look at a range of stories which contain contrasting feelings: death and resurrection, welcome and rejection.

Other useful passages

The welcome of the crowd on Palm Sunday and the rejection of Jesus on Good Friday, Book 3, pages 47, 48.

The loyalty professed by Peter can be contrasted with the betrayal, Book 1, page 52.

The greed of the "Rich Fool", Book 1, page 63, and the generosity of the widow who shared her last meal, Book 1, page 64.

The lack of concern shown by the priest and Levite and the practical care shown by the Good Samaritan, Book 3, page 19.

Death and resurrection, Book 3, pages 49–50, 51.

"The Sheep and the Goats", Book 3, page 18.

The whole section entitled "Change", pages 63–68.

Contrasts are also found in the following stories: "Martha and Mary", Book 1, page 10, "Jonah Runs Away", Book 1, page 96–97, and "Jonah gets Cross", Book 1, page 82, "The Unforgiving Servant", Book 1, page 78, "The Two Sons", Book 1, page 95, and "The Two Houses", Book 1, page 99.

Cross–curricular links

English
- Create "mind maps" of happy and sad thoughts and other contrasts. (3)
- Read *Burglar Bill* by J Ahlberg (Heinemann, 1979). Write a report/story from the opposite point of view. (2, 3)
- Write poems starting: Happiness is… Sorrow is… These can be done on biblical stories if children would rather not explore their own thoughts. (3)

Science and Technology
- Investigate various opposites in weather: hot and cold, windy and calm, wet and dry. Record weather patterns over a period of time and explore patterns and trends which emerge. (SAT 1, 4)
- Investigate how magnets attract and repel. Make a simple electro–magnet. Incorporate your magnet into a working model to demonstrate attracting and repelling. (1, 4) (GAT 3)

Art
- Explore hot and cold colours: investigate the colour wheels. Mix secondary and tertiary colours from primary colours. (1)
- Create silhouettes and cameos: black on white, white on black. (1)
- Make clay faces in pairs with opposite expressions. (1)

Music
- Investigate percussion instruments. Some make sharp, sudden sounds. Others make long sustained notes, why? Write a graphic score to illustrate this. Listen to music with different dynamics such as *Carmina Burana* by Carl Orff. (1, 2)

PE/Dance
- Mirror images: copy a partner's movements as if you were a reflection. Then try it standing behind rather than in front. (KS 1/2)

- Create a sequence of movements involving opposites: low/high, slow/quick, etc. (KS 1/2)
- Explore movements with different moods: joyful, sad, excited, angry. (KS 1/2)

Geography
- Look at patterns of night and day and the seasons — link this with science. (3) (SAT 4)
- Why are some countries always hot or always cold? Why are some wet and others dry? Find out what conditions contribute towards climatic regions. (3)
- Compare in detail two settlements such as old and new towns, a city and a village. (2, 3, 4, 5)

History
- Using the unit "The Victorians", compare and contrast different areas of society with today. What positive things can be learnt from Victorian society? Extracts from literature can be used for this: *The Little Princess* by F. Hodgson Burnett (Puffin, 1984). *Oliver Twist* and *David Copperfield* by C Dickens (Penguin, 1969), *Larkrise to Candleford* by Flora Thompson (Penguin, 1989). (1, 2, 3) (EAT 2)

Personal and Social Education
- Discuss a local issue such as a bypass or a new development. Role–play/debate opposite viewpoints. Similar issues could be discussed for health education such as smoking. (EAT 1)

Mathematics
- Various opposites can be explored in maths: bigger and smaller, more and less, odd and even numbers, whole and part numbers, two–dimensional and three–dimensional shapes, round and angular, symmetrical and non–symmetrical. Explore these at whatever level of thinking is appropriate for the age group. (1, 2, 3, 4)

THE TEN LEPERS
Luke 17.11–19 ▶ *page 32*

A Christian perspective
Despite their desperate call for help, most of the people healed forgot to say thank you. Saying thank you is an important element in prayer. Christians believe all things come from God, including healing, and therefore gratitude is due to him.

Points of interest
1. The man with leprosy who thanked Jesus was a Samaritan, a group hated by the Jews because

they were of mixed origins (not true Jews) and because they worshipped in a way of which the Jews did not approve. There was also long–standing bad feeling between Jews and Samaritans for political reasons. The group of leprosy sufferers was mixed, Jews and Samaritans.
2. Leprosy was a blanket word which covered many skin diseases, a fact which early Israelite law recognized. Once leprosy was diagnosed (by the priest) the person was isolated, and food was

left for them outside the village, although we now know that leprosy is not very contagious. It was a very lonely life and sometimes sufferers banded together.

3. The priest acted as the doctor of the community. The Law stated that sufferers had to show themselves to the priest to prove they had been cured. Such a public demonstration would also have eased their way back into the community, for otherwise people may have been wary of them.

4. Kneeling was a mark of respect.

NABOTH'S VINEYARD
ELIJAH: EPISODE 4
1 Kings 21 ▶ *page 33*

A Christian perspective

This is a story of injustice by default: Ahab did not stop wrong from happening when it was in his power to do so. To Jezebel, Naboth was just a peasant farmer who could be disposed of. To God, he was one of his people, valued and loved. During the story, four of the Ten Commandments are broken: for the wrongdoers are guilty of envy, theft, murder, and bearing false witness.

In Israel the kings were only kings under God. The king was never above the law as Elijah's condemnation shows. The king was meant to administer God's laws, not pervert them for his own ends. God is described as a God of justice in the Bible. Naboth would not be allowed to die unnoticed. Wrong would not go unchallenged.

Points of interest

1. Jezebel would have been used to Phoenician laws (modern Lebanon), hence her surprise that Ahab initially accepted Naboth's refusal. She also assumed the property of a 'criminal' reverted to the crown, which was not so in Israel.

2. Land was not seen as a personal possession: it was given by God and held "on lease" for him. It also secured a living for future generations. The Israelites were told not to sell their land, hence Naboth's refusal.

3. The elders of a village or town administered justice. It was strictly forbidden to pervert justice by accepting a bribe or bringing false charges. Anyone who brought a false accusation was condemned to suffer the penalty the innocent party would have suffered if convicted.

THE DEATH OF JOHN THE BAPTIST
Matthew 14.1–12 ▶ *page 34*

A Christian perspective

The main point of this story is the bravery of John, who did not mince his words even though he knew he would suffer for it. Kings were not considered to be above God's Law, as King Ahab had found out earlier when Elijah condemned him for killing Naboth (page 33). It is also a story of calculated hatred on the part of Herod's wife.

Points of interest

1. This is not the same Herod who tried to kill baby Jesus. This is Herod Antipas, his son. Herodias, Herod's wife, had already been married to his half–brother, so it was illegal for Herod to marry her.

2. It was very unusual for a Jewish girl, particularly a princess, to dance before men, but given the reputation of Herod's court, not impossible.

3. John the Baptist was beheaded in the prison of Machaerus on the Dead Sea. Execution by beheading was not allowed in Jewish law.

4. John was very popular and Herod was superstitious about killing a prophet. When Herod suffered defeat in AD 36, the people thought it was punishment for the way he treated John the Baptist.

PAUL'S HYMN OF LOVE
1 Corinthians 13 ▶ *page 35*

A Christian perspective

The Greeks had four words for love, the English have to make do with one that covers everything from Heaven to Hollywood. The Greek word used here is agape, which is selfless love, a love which gives even if the person loving gets nothing in return. This passage is about loving behaviour. In biblical thought, love is more than an emotion, it also involves the will. It is how a person behaves, not just how they feel at that moment.

Paul admits that he understands little and that understanding God is like looking in a dim mirror. Mirrors then were made of polished metal, so the image was not clear. Christians believe that one day they will see God "face to face": one day there will be nothing to hinder the relationship.

Points of interest

The description of love:
1. Kind: this is actively relieving suffering — practical love.

2. Is not proud: this means not being puffed up with your own importance. There is a right sort of pride and a wrong sort. The type that is condemned is self–centred and conceited.
3. Is not rude: this is about behaviour, not swear–words. It is telling people to use appropriate behaviour towards others.
4. Does not grow angry quickly: God is described as being "slow to anger".
5. Love keeps no record of wrongs: the Bible says that God hides people's wrongs, he buries them beneath the sea so they can't be seen. People are asked to treat each other in the same way.
6. Hope: hope is certain because it is grounded in God. It is not wishful thinking.
7. Faith: having faith is seen as living according to unseen realities.
8. Love is defined as the highest virtue because the Bible sums up God's character in the description "God is love".

JAIRUS' DAUGHTER
Mark 5.21–43 ▶ *page 36*

A Christian perspective
For Christians, this story demonstrates Jesus' power over death: other miracles demonstrate his power over disease, troubled minds and nature. It was the beginning of the reversal — the rolling back of all those things that spoil life.

Both miracles required faith. Miracles are not seen as magic tricks: they take place as part of a relationship. Jesus does not let the woman go away with the idea that just a "magical" touch has cured her.

Points of interest
1. Jairus highly values his daughter. All children were highly valued, though boys had a special place in Middle Eastern society. The little girl was twelve, just of marriageable age.
2. There would have been professional mourners as well as family and friends at the house. Even in the poorest house, two flutes and a wailing woman would have been used.
3. The woman touched "the edge of Jesus' garment". This could have been one of the four tassels that Jewish men wore.

Teacher resource

Fuelled

Fuelled
by a million
man–made
wings of fire—
the rocket tore a tunnel
through the sky—
and everybody cheered.

Fuelled
only by a thought from God—
the seedling
urged its way
through the thickness of black—
and as it pierced
the heavy ceiling of the soil—
and launched itself
up into outer space—
no
one
even
clapped.

Marcie Hans

The Ten Lepers

Luke 17.11–19

The ten men hurried down the road, jostling each other in their eagerness to be first. Jesus had sent them to the priests. "Perhaps we'll be healed by the time we get there," they were all thinking.

How wonderful it would be if they were healed!

Their life was so lonely and unhappy. As soon as their friends and families had found out that these men had leprosy, they had thrown them out. "We don't want to catch it!" they'd shouted. "Go and live with the other people like you in the caves." For all people with leprosy had to live away from the villages, in caves or rough shelters, relying on other people for food. Wherever they went, other people ran away from them.

That day, they'd seen Jesus walking towards the village. They had quickly decided to ask him to cure them. Even they, in their lonely life, had heard that he could heal people. They had stood as near to the road as they had dared and shouted to him: "Jesus! Please heal us!"

Now, as they hurried to the priests, first one, then another realized that his skin was perfect again. They were healed! Nine of them rushed on. They knew they couldn't go back to their families until the priests had declared they were cured. But the tenth one, a Samaritan, stopped. He must say thank you! He rushed back to Jesus. He threw himself on to his knees in front of him and thanked him. "Thank God!" he shouted, "I'm healed! Thank you Jesus, thank you!"

Jesus looked around. "Where are the others?" he asked. "Weren't there ten of you altogether?" Then, looking down at the man, he said, "Go to the priests now; you are healed because you believed in me."

But that man was the only one who came to say thank you.

RESOURCE BANK 2: OPPOSITES

Naboth's Vineyard

ELIJAH: EPISODE 4

1 Kings 21

Next to King Ahab's palace, there was a vineyard belonging to a man called Naboth. One day, Ahab had an idea. "If I owned that vineyard," he thought, "I could have it made into a vegetable garden. It would be really handy just there." So he went to Naboth and offered to buy it, or to exchange it for one in a different place.

But Naboth didn't want to lose it. "My family has owned this land for years and years. I'll keep it," he told the astonished king.

Ahab was furious. How dare the man refuse the king anything? He went home, lay on his bed and sulked! He even refused to eat anything. When his wife Jezebel came in and found out why he was upset, she laughed at him. "Come on!" she jeered. "You are the king. You and I — we can do just what we like."

Then she carried out a cruel plot against Naboth. She wrote to the rulers of Naboth's city, using the king's own seal to mark the letter, so they thought the orders came from Ahab. "Find some people to make false accusations against Naboth and have him killed," she wrote — and that is what happened.

When she heard Naboth was dead, Jezebel hurried to her husband. "You have your garden," she announced. "Naboth is dead!" Ahab was so pleased to get the land. Now he could plan his new garden.

Soon afterwards, Elijah came to see the king. "What do you want?" Ahab asked him rudely.

"God has sent me to tell you that he knows about the evil things you have done," Elijah replied. "He knows that Naboth is dead. God will see that justice is done on Naboth's behalf."

The Death of John the Baptist

Matthew 14.1–12

King Herod did not know what to do about John the Baptist. He had soon had him thrown into prison when he heard that John had been criticizing him for marrying his brother's wife. John the Baptist said openly that their marriage was wrong. Herod's wife, Herodias, was so angry that she wanted John killed. But Herod was afraid to do that. He knew how popular John was: he didn't want to cause any riots, or he could be in trouble himself with the Romans. In any case, he liked listening to John when he spoke about God, even though he didn't understand a lot of it. So John stayed in prison, Herodias continued to beg for his death — and Herod tried to keep everyone happy.

One night, at one of Herod's great banquets, Herodias' daughter danced for her stepfather and his guests. Herod saw that the guests enjoyed her dancing, and he was pleased with her, too. He sent for her. "Ask me for anything you want," he told her, "as a reward for your dancing."

"Thank you, sir," she replied, "but could I ask my mother for her advice first?"

Herodias realized at once that this was her chance. "Ask for the death of John the Baptist," she told her daughter.

Herod was dismayed. All his guests had heard his promise to the girl. He couldn't refuse her request now. He sent the executioner to John's cell and John the Baptist was killed. When his followers heard about what had happened, they took away his body, to bury it properly.

Jesus was upset when he heard the news. John was a relative of his, and he had been helping Jesus by his teaching. It was John who had baptized Jesus himself, and had told people about him. Now he had been killed because of his bravery in speaking out against Herod.

Paul's Hymn of Love

1 Corinthians 13

Love is all–important. No matter how clever or gifted or full of faith I am, no matter how generous or brave, if there is no love in me, my life is like an empty, meaningless noise and I can achieve nothing.

Love is patient and kind. It does not feel envious of others. Love behaves well towards other people. It does not boast and is not proud. Love does not grow angry quickly or easily, and keeps no record of the wrongs other people have done. Love is not happy at the sight of wrongdoing: rather it rejoices in those things which are good and true. Love always take care of others and always believes the best. Love carries on hoping and does not give up easily.

For love never fails. Other things are only temporary and needed for only a short time. But love goes on and on. When I was a child, I thought and reasoned like a child but now I am grown–up I have given up childish things. Life now is like looking through a dim mirror but one day everything will be clear. One day I shall know God fully, even as he knows and understands me completely. Three things last in life: faith, hope and love — but the greatest is love.

Jairus' Daughter

Mark 5.21–43

Peter: When we arrived back in Capernaum, there was a big crowd of people waiting for us already: they'd heard we were coming. Jesus was just beginning to talk to them when a man pushed his way through and knelt in front of him. I recognized him as Jairus, a ruler of the synagogue — an important man in Capernaum. He looked up at Jesus imploringly.

"My little daughter is dying! Please come home with me Jesus, so that you can heal her," he begged. Jesus agreed, and we set off.

It was slow going. The crowds couldn't get out of our way in the narrow streets, and everyone was trying to stay near Jesus anyway. Suddenly Jesus stopped. He looked around puzzled. "Someone touched me," he said.

I looked at the people milling around. I should think at least twenty people had touched him: we couldn't help it in the crush. I began to explain this to him, but he interrupted me with, "No! I mean that someone has touched me because they wanted me to heal them."

Then a woman came forward. She looked pale and frightened. She had been trying to get away, I think, but had realized that Jesus was waiting for her. She knelt down in front of him. "I touched you, master," she admitted. Then she explained that she had been ill for many years, and no doctor had been able to cure her, although she had spent all her money on them. She told him she had heard about the way he had healed people. "I knew that if I could just touch you — even if it was only the edge of your cloak — I would be healed," she ended simply. Jesus smiled at her. "You are healed because you believed in me," he explained. "Go home now, and begin to live a normal life."

All this time, Jairus had been waiting impatiently. Now we began to struggle through the crowd again. But then Jairus stopped. One of his servants had come to meet him. "I'm sorry, Jairus," he said. "Your daughter is dead. Don't bother Jesus any longer."

Jairus was really upset. He turned to Jesus, but Jesus spoke first. "Don't worry," he said. "Let's carry on." As we drew near to Jairus' house, we could hear the women there crying. We hurried in, and Jesus told them to stop their mourning. "The little girl is asleep, but I can waken her," he said. They all laughed at him: they knew perfectly well that the child was dead.

We went into the child's room. Jesus walked over to the bed, and bent down. He took her hand in his, and said, "Get up little girl!" And the girl opened her eyes and stretched. She saw her mother and father, jumped off the bed and went to them. It was lovely to see their faces as they held her! They hugged her, and then looked at her as if to make sure she was all right — and then they hugged her again. Jesus watched them with a smile on his face. Then he said, "Get her something to eat, she's hungry!" He told them, too, to keep what had happened a secret. Then we left them to enjoy being together.

RESOURCE BANK 2: OPPOSITES

Thank You

Read the story of "The Ten Lepers" on page 32.

Only one came back to say thank you, in sharp contrast to the nine who forgot.

Listen to the poem "Fuelled".

Think about it

Why do you think the nine lepers forgot to say thank you? Why do you think people often forget to say thank you for the "everyday" miracles?

Word Bank

Read the passage called "Paul's Hymn of Love" on page 35.

Activity

- Write a list of the main words used in this passage.

  Example: Boastful, Kind, Proud, etc.

- Each person should choose one word to investigate, and write it on a piece of card.

- Use a dictionary to find out the various meanings of the word. Write these meanings on the back of the card.

- Construct a heart shape out of card and cut it out. How could you display the various words from the "Hymn of Love" so that people will be able to read both the words and the meaning?

Example:

On Trial

Read the story of "Naboth's Vineyard" on page 33.

Activity

- If you were in the Police in the time of Naboth whom would you arrest for this crime and whom would you put on trial?

- Discuss this with some friends.

- Decide whom you would prosecute.

- Prepare your case against the accused and write it up.

Think about it

Do you think the jury would find the accused "guilty" or "not guilty"? Give a reason for your answer.

Opposites

Choose two stories which contain opposites.

Activity

• Can you design a pair of symbols which will express the opposites in behaviour expressed in these stories?

Example:

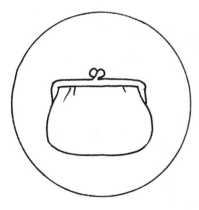

The Rich Fool (Book 1, page 63)   The Widow's Gift (page 105)

• Things to think about: size, colour, shape, pattern.

• How could you display your pair of symbols?

Think about it

Christians believe that good and evil are opposites but they are not equally strong. They believe good is stronger than evil.

PROMISES

Understanding the biblical ideas

Throughout the Bible, God is described as entering into agreements with humanity, and standing by those agreements or promises. These are not, however, contracts between two equal partners. The agreement is always at God's initiative: he is the one who offers the contract and makes the promise. The word agreement or "covenant" is sometimes translated as "Testament" (as in "Last Will and Testament") — hence the Old Testament (agreement) and the New Testament (agreement).

1. The first agreement is with Noah. Never again would God flood the earth, and nature would always be stable: summer and winter, seedtime and harvest would not cease. The sign of this covenant was a rainbow.
2. The next agreement is with Abraham, and God promises him descendants and land. The seal of this agreement is the sign of circumcision. The partial fulfilment of Abraham's promise came with the birth of Isaac, but the land did not come until Moses' day.
3. The promise to Moses was that Israel would be God's special people and he would be their God. The Law was the out–working of this agreement. God would dwell with them and he would give them their own land.
4. David was promised the throne of Israel. He had to wait a long time before he became king, but God promised that the throne would stay in his family.
5. The promise of a special king or Messiah is scattered throughout the prophets. This special king would be a descendant of David.
6. With Jeremiah comes the promise of a New Covenant, one written on the heart of each individual: a promise that one day the relationship will change, as people will want to serve God from the heart.
7. The promises of the New Testament are many: Jesus promises that he will never turn anyone away, that he will always be with them, even to the end of the world, and that one day the whole earth will know God and be at peace.

The promises of God start with a very wide application: Noah's is with the world, Abraham's and Moses' with a nation, David's with a dynasty. Finally, the promises centre on one person, the Messiah. After that they widen again to the Jews, the Gentiles (non–Jews), and the whole earth.

Introducing the passages

Discuss promises with the children. What sort of promises do we make? What sort of promises are made to us? Do people always keep their promises? Do we always keep ours? What sometimes stops people from keeping their promises? Look at formal promises and contracts.

Use the cycle of the seasons to introduce Noah.

Use a land contract to introduce Abraham and Moses. If possible, bring in a copy of a contract.

Talk about behaviour contracts. Draw up some as an example. Look at the Law as the Israelites' side of the agreement.

Explore the ways in which rulers are chosen and read the story of David.

Discuss how we dream of things we would like for the future. Introduce the promises for the future included in this section.

Other useful passages

"Jesus Says Goodbye", Book 3, page 52. This story is about the promise of the Holy Spirit.

"Hannah's Precious Gift", page 104. In this story, Hannah makes a vow, or an agreement with God which she keeps.

"Ruth and Naomi", Book 1, page 5. In this story Ruth vows to stand by Naomi.

"The Ten Commandments", page 21. God promises that Israel will be his special people.

"Dry Bones", Book 3, page 94. In this story God promises that he will give the people hope and a future.

Cross–curricular links

English

- Think about promises you have made or have been made to you — were they kept or broken? Which do you remember and why? (1)
- Discuss keeping your word. Write a poem to show your feelings when someone lets you down. (1, 3)
- Discuss the oaths taken by witnesses in court (and perjury). Look at promises made by members of a group such as Girl Guides: how difficult or easy is it to keep these promises? A promise should never be taken lightly. (1, 2)
- Perform a story/personal news report, etc., for younger children about an incident where a promise has/has not been kept. It could be presented in dramatic, book or video form. (1, 3)
- Write Noah's story from the point of view of one of the animals. (3)
- Select one of the other stories of promise, invent an animal that could have been present and write the story from the animal's point of view. You could be a duck on the River Nile in the story of Moses, or a mouse in Abraham's tent. (3)
- Perform part of the miracle play "The Deluge" adapted from the medieval original. This can be found in *Miracle Plays* by A Malcolmson (Constable, 1960). (EAT 1, 2)

Mathematics

- Look at bank notes which carry the words — "I promise to pay the bearer on demand the sum of…" Look at currency, cheques and cheque cards, and the role of keeping promises to pay. (2)

Personal and Social Education

- Look at the promises made in advertising. Examine specific advertisements. How are the promises made: through speech, through images, through subtle linking of ideas? Do they live up to their promises? Design a set of ethical rules for advertising which safeguards the customer against false promises. (EAT 1, 2, 3)

Science

- God's agreement with Noah was that the earth would never be flooded again, nature would be stable, summer and winter, seedtime and harvest would not cease. Look at the various patterns in seasons across the world. Has human activity affected seedtime/harvest? (2, 3, 4)
- Explore light and the nature of colour. Why do rainbows happen? (4)

Art

- Create a large two–dimensional map of the Holy land reaching as far as Egypt and Persia (modern Iran). Use various means of printing for the different parts of the map. For example: sponge printing for the sea, block printing for the mountains. Make separate figures of Moses, Abraham and Sarah and mark their wanderings on the map. (1)

PE/Dance

- Using the music of Boney M, "By the Rivers of Babylon", dance the feelings of the Israelites over captivity and the second exodus back to the Promised Land. Show in your movements how they must have felt before, during, and at the end of that journey. The music can be found in *Alleluya* (A & C Black). (KS 1/2)
- Express the character of different animals in the ark through dance. (KS 1/2)

Music

- Listen to or perform the music *Captain Noah and his Floating Zoo* by J Horovitz and M Flanders (Novello) or *The History of the Flood* by D Lord (OUP). Listen to parts of *Noye's Fludde* by Britten. (1, 2)
- Make up short pieces of music which express the character of different animals in the ark. (1)
- Explore "spirituals" such as "Go Down Moses" which celebrate some of the stories in this section. (1, 2)

NOAH
Genesis 6.9–9.17 ▶ *page 45*

A Christian perspective

The story of Noah is one of judgement, rescue, promise, and a fresh start. It is a difficult subject and needs handling very carefully. Judgement has two sides, positive and negative. Positively it is the defence of the victims. Negatively it is the punishment of the wrongdoer. In this story people fulfil both roles: they are the victims and the perpetrators of violence, so only Noah and his family are spared.

There are two promises: firstly that God will never again seek this solution to evil; and secondly that there will always be stability in nature.

The promise concerning the seasons does not mean there will never be a bad harvest. It means that nature will be stable and fruitful. People will know when to plant and reap because there will be regular seasons.

Points of interest

1. This first promise to Noah concerns the whole earth. The promises are progressively narrowed after this: one nation (Israel), one dynasty (David's), one person (the Messiah).
2. The forty days of rain is a symbolic number. The Israelites were forty years in the wilderness. Jesus was forty days in the desert.
3. The word translated as "rainbow" literally means "bow of war". The sign means that God has set aside his bow, his anger.

ABRAHAM

Genesis 12.1–3; 15; 17.15–22; 18.1–15; 21.1–8
▶ *page 47*

A Christian perspective

In this story, Abraham and Sarah were given two promises which they find extremely difficult to believe. They were nomads, and God told them they would one day have a land of their own. They were old, and God promised them children. Christians emphasize the faith that it took for Abraham and Sarah to believe these promises, they believe it was important that the founders of the nation were people who trusted God.

Points on interest

1. Abraham came from the region of Ur, a highly civilized area of Mesopotamia (in modern Iraq).
2. Abraham and Sarah both laughed (Abraham on an earlier occasion) when they were promised a child. When the child was eventually born, he was called "Issac" which means "laughter".
3. Not having children was as great a sorrow in the ancient world as it is today. If a woman did not bear her husband children, a man was allowed to take a second wife. Children were important: through them, life went on.
4. Hospitality was extremely important. There were no instant eating places in the ancient world. Often a tent was pitched facing the direction from which visitors might come.
5. The angels represent God. Light is sometimes associated with angels, but they are not the white–clad beings of Victorian paintings. They arrive as good strangers with messages from God.

MOSES: PROMISES START TO COME TRUE

MOSES: EPISODE 4
Exodus 5–12.39 ▶ *page 49*

A Christian perspective

God had told Abraham that his people would be enslaved but that he would rescue them and bring them into their own land. For the Israelites, the escape from Egypt was the beginning of the fulfilment of that promise. It is also a story of rescue, freedom, and judgement.

Points of interest

1. The ten plagues are remembered each year at the Passover when ten drops of wine are split. Lamb is eaten as a reminder of the way the firstborn were saved.
2. The first–born was the special child, the one who would inherit. Each first–born son belonged to God as a symbol that all life really came from him. Not until the Egyptians felt the loss of their children as the Hebrew slaves had done, did Pharaoh let the people go.
3. Rameses II was succeeded by Meneptah who was not his eldest son. It may have been Meneptah's brother who died in this incident.

DAVID IS CHOSEN TO BE KING

DAVID: EPISODE 1
1 Samuel 16.1–13 ▶ *page 51*

A Christian perspective

Christians believe that God looks on the inside. In this story, God chooses the person other people had discounted because he looked beyond the outward impression.

Points of interest

1. David was promised the throne but he did not try to grab the kingship by force. Several times he could have killed Saul but didn't.
2. Samuel anointed David: that was the act by which kings were designated. Oil was used at Queen Elizabeth II's coronation. The special king, or Messiah, was descended from David and the very word "messiah" means "anointed".
3. Saul has been the first king of Israel. Samuel had been reluctant to give the nation a king because God was their king. The people, however, wanted to be like other nations and God had told Samuel to go ahead and anoint Saul. Saul had been a good leader, defeating Israel's enemies and initially ruling the people well, but later he

was rejected as king, although he kept the throne until his death.

PROMISES FOR THE FUTURE

Isaiah 9.6–7; Jeremiah 31.31–34, 36; Matthew 28.20 ▶ *page 52*

A Christian perspective

The promise of the Messiah and of a new age when justice and peace would rule were a hope that was kept alive in Israel for hundreds of years. In Jesus' time, people expected a descendant of David to arrive to start this new age of justice. Christians believe that Jesus was that long–expected king.

The New Agreement: the Bible describes God making various agreements with the Israelites: with Noah, Abraham, Moses and the people, and with David. The prophets also speak of a new agreement, some time in the future when the Law will be written on the heart: a time when people will want to enter into friendship with God and to live as he wants them to. Christians interpret the new agreement as starting with Jesus.

The psalmist describes the continuing presence of God in Psalm 139 (Book 1, page 34). The idea of God's presence was not new. Here Jesus is confirming the Old Testament and adding that "he" will be present. Christians believe God showed what he was like in Jesus. When Christians think about having God present with them, they believe they know a little of what he is like because of Jesus.

Noah

Genesis 6.9–9.17

How good the land looked! The colours of the grass and the flowers were so bright and varied! Noah felt the solid earth under his feet. He bent down and let a handful of soil slip through his fingers. They could grow good crops here. He listened to the birds, free at last, singing out their happiness as they perched in the bushes and trees or swooped joyously in the clear air. Most of the animals had already moved off, out of sight. Once out of the ark, some had raced, bucking and leaping, over the grassy plains. The slower ones had scurried after them, stretching their legs and delighting in the wide spaces, before settling down to eat the fresh green grass, or to pluck the tender young leaves and shoots and bushes. Now, most had scattered over the land, finding new territories for themselves. Noah was old, but he felt like running too. There was so much space! It was good to be out in the fresh air, surrounded by all the things he had once taken for granted, but which he had lost for so long — the rivers, the mountains, the grass. Noah, his family, and all the animals had been penned up in the ark for nearly a year. He thought about the last time he had stood on the earth like this. How long ago it seemed.

Noah remembered the hard work, all the family struggling to finish the great boat, for which God had given him such detailed plans. He remembered the jeers of his neighbours: "Noah must be mad! Why is he building that monstrosity?" He had tried to explain to them, but they wouldn't listen. He remembered the frightening moment when God had firmly closed the ark's door, and they were inside — he and his family, shut in with every kind of animal and bird.

"God has promised to look after us. We'll be all right," he had told his wife and sons. But it had still been frightening when the rain went on and on, and first the fields, then the hills, and then the mountains themselves had disappeared under the water.

"I have to make a new start on the earth," God had told him. "The people here have been so evil. They are spoiling my beautiful world and I cannot bear to see how they hurt each other. But I will save you and your family."

Then, finally the rain had stopped. In the ark, they waited and waited for the great flood to go down.

Then, at last, the dove which Noah had sent out came back with a little sprig of green leaves. "Look!" Noah had shouted to his family. "She's found an olive tree!" So they had known that soon they could leave the ark. Each day they watched the level of the water. Each day more and more land reappeared. It dried out in the sun and grass began to grow again. The world seemed to come back to life before their eyes.

Now, Noah heard his sons calling him. They had finished building the altar. It was time to praise God for this new beginning, to thank him for keeping them all safe. Noah walked over to his family. Together they knelt and spoke to God.

God had something to say to them too. As the earth had grown green again, God looked at its beauty. Now he heard Noah's prayers, and he made this promise: "For as long as the earth lasts, there will always be a time for sowing,

Noah — continued

and a time for reaping: there will be warmth and cold, summer and winter, and day and night."

Then God made another promise to Noah and his family. "Never again will I send a great flood to cover all the earth. Look! I've set a rainbow in the sky. Do you see it? Whenever you see its beauty among the rain clouds, you are to remember my promise." And the rainbow arched over the beautiful earth.

Abraham

Genesis 12.1–3; 15; 17.15–22;18.1–15; 21.1–8

Abraham sat outside his tent, sheltering under a tree from the fierce heat of the sun. It was midday, time to rest. He looked out over the countryside. "This will be your land," God had told him. "Travel through it from one end to the other. Look to the North, to the West, to the South and to the East: it is all for you and your descendants."

It was a good land, a rich fertile land. Abraham had travelled many miles since he was a boy in the great city of Ur. He had trekked to Haran with his father, and there he had remained until God first spoke to him about this new land, telling him to travel on until he found it. So Abraham had gathered together all his flocks and herds of animals, packed up his belongings, folded up the tents in which they lived, and travelled to an unknown country with Sarah his wife and his nephew Lot.

Many things had happened since then. They had even travelled over to Egypt to obtain food during a famine. Many years had passed, but Abraham still believed in God's promise: one day, his family would fill this land. One day it would be their own possession instead of just somewhere to camp as they travelled through it.

But God had made another promise, all those years ago to Abraham and Sarah. "You will have as many descendants as there are stars in the sky. There will be so many that it will be as easy to count the grains of dust on the earth as it will be to count your descendants." Abraham believed that God would keep this promise too, although he and Sarah were already old.

Abraham closed his eyes and imagined what it would be like to have a child living in the tent with them, riding on his shoulders to look at the flocks, running in and out to show Sarah little treasures he had found. Abraham realized with a start that he could hear voices. He looked up and saw three strangers coming. Quickly he went to greet them, his mind racing: what food was available to offer them? He bowed to them, and asked them to join him for a meal. He settled them in the shade, brought water for their feet, and hurried to Sarah, asking her to prepare the food. Soon, he stood watching them eat.

"Where is your wife, Sarah?" one asked.

Abraham was surprised. "She's in the tent," he answered.

"About this time next year," the stranger told him, "Sarah will have a baby son."

Now Sarah, who was listening inside the tent, laughed to herself. "I'm far too old to have a son now," she said to herself.

The stranger knew she had laughed, and said. "Why is Sarah laughing? Doesn't she know that the Lord can do anything?"

Sarah was frightened. Who could these men be? They seemed to know all about her.

Eventually the three men departed, leaving Sarah both frightened and hopeful. She watched them walk away, down the road, Abraham accompanying them. "Will I really have a child?" she wondered. "After all these years?"

Abraham — continued

Soon afterwards, Sarah knew the answer herself, and about a year after the strangers' visit, she held her new baby, Issac, thanking God that he had kept his promise. Now Abraham and Sarah had a new land, and a family.

RESOURCE BANK 2: PROMISES

Moses: Promises Start to Come True

MOSES: EPISODE 4

Exodus 5—12.39

Pharaoh was furious! Who did these two Hebrew slaves think they were? What were their names? Yes, Moses and Aaron. How dare they come in here and tell him that the Hebrew God wanted his people to go and worship him in the desert? "These people are my slaves. They do as I say!" he thundered. "If they've got time to listen to rubbish like this, then they've not got enough work to do! We'll make them work even harder. Let me see…Yes, I know what to do. Stop giving them the straw with which to make the bricks. Let them gather their own. That will keep them busy!"

So the poor Hebrew slaves had even more work to do. "We need more time!" they complained.

"No!" shouted Pharaoh. "We want the same number of bricks in the same length of time. You're just lazy!"

It was impossible! Poor Aaron and Moses got the blame. "You've made things worse for us, not better," the Hebrews moaned.

Moses spoke to God. "Why is this happening, Lord? What are we to do?"

"I will force Pharaoh to let you leave his country," God said "I am the Lord. I have always been the Hebrews' God, and I will rescue them and bring them into their new country. I will perform many wonderful things — things that seem impossible to men. But, sadly, Pharaoh will not obey me until his own people have suffered greatly. Then, my people will leave Egypt. This is what you are to do, Moses." And God told Moses what to do and say.

Moses had many meetings with Pharaoh over the next weeks. He continually warned him about the awful events that would occur if he did not let the Hebrew slaves leave the country. Each time it happened just as God had told Moses to predict. The waters of the Nile turned into blood! Then frogs covered the land: they were everywhere! Great swarms of gnats and flies appeared. The Egyptians' animals died. Then all the Egyptians were covered with horrible sores. How ill they all felt! Next, a terrible hailstorm beat down on the land and flattened all the Egyptians' crops. Swarms of locusts came down on Egypt and ate all the trees and plants they could find. Then for three whole days, the sun did not shine. That was frightening! The Egyptians looked over to Goshen, the part of Egypt where the Hebrews lived. "Look!" they said. "They have light!"

"Yes, and their animals did not die either."

"That's right — and the flies and hail didn't touch them," the Egyptians complained.

Then Pharaoh did agree to let the Hebrew slaves go. "But he's said that before," said the Hebrews. "He'll change his mind again." And they were right.

So God said to Moses, "Now there is only one trouble left for Egypt. Soon Pharaoh will beg you to go." He gave Moses one last message for Pharaoh. "At 12 o'clock tonight, every first-born son in every family in Egypt — from

Pharaoh's down to the poorest — will die. The Egyptians will be heartbroken, but no Hebrew child will be harmed at all."

Then God told Moses that the Hebews were to get ready a special meal. They were to prepare special food, including a lamb. Some of the blood from this lamb was to be painted on the doorframe of each house. This would be a sign that God's people lived there. They were to call this meal the Passover Meal, because death would "pass over" these houses. The people did all that God had told them to do. That night, they ate their special food and waited to see what God would do.

David is Chosen to be King

DAVID: EPISODE 1

1 Samuel 16.1–13

Samuel paused for a rest on the hill overlooking the village. He was an old man now, and the journey to Bethlehem had tired him. He was also a little unhappy and puzzled. "What will the next king be like?" he wondered. He sighed. He could remember so well the time when he had anointed Israel's first king, Saul, all those years ago. He had never really wanted a king, but the people had been so determined that Israel should have a king and be like the other nations. Saul had been a good king at first, and he was a good soldier, but he had changed. He had disobeyed God and now another king would have to be chosen.

"So here I am," thought Samuel. "Somewhere down there, one of Jesse's sons is to be the new king." Then he prayed, "Help me listen carefully to you, God, so that I choose the man you want as king of Israel."

Once in the village, Samuel spoke to Jesse: "I have come here to worship God," he told him, "and I want you and your sons to join me."

Jesse hurried off proudly to fetch his sons. Soon, he was back in front of Samuel, introducing his eldest son. Samuel looked at the young man closely. "How strong and tall he looks!" he was thinking. "Surely this is the man God has chosen!"

But God told him, "No Samuel. He is not the man I want. You are thinking about his appearance. But I don't care what people look like. I care about what people are really like inside. I can see whether they are brave and wise, and whether they really love me." So Samuel listened to what God was saying while Jesse introduced six more of his sons to him. But God did not choose any of them.

In the end, Samuel said, "You must have another son, surely?"

"Well, yes," Jesse said reluctantly. "There's David, the youngest, but he's in the fields, looking after the sheep."

"I want to see him," Samuel said.

So David came down to the village. As soon as Samuel saw him, he heard God saying, "Yes! This is the one I have chosen. Anoint him!"

And Samuel poured the oil over David's head, in front of David's astonished family. So Samuel showed that David was special to God, and that God was with him. Jesse and his other sons looked on in amazement. David was the youngest and smallest, and none of them thought much of him at all. What was so special about him? But David just went back to his work.

Promises for the Future

Isaiah 9.6–7; Jeremiah 31.31–34; Matthew 28.20

The Promise of a Special King (Messiah)
A child will be born to us,
A son will be given to us.
He will be our ruler and he will be called
Wonderful Counsellor, Mighty God,
Everlasting Father, Prince of Peace.
He will rule in peace and justice forever.
(Isaiah 9.6–7)

The Promise of a New Agreement
"The time will come when I will make a new agreement with my people. In my new agreement, I will place my law deep within them. They will have my love inside their hearts and minds. I myself will help them keep their promises to me. I will be their God, and they will be my people. They will not learn about me just from other people: they will all be able to know me for themselves — all of them, the least as well as the most powerful, for I will forgive all their sins. I will not even remember what they did wrong!

"This promise will last as long as the earth endures." (Jeremiah 31.31–34)

The Continuing Presence of God
Just before he left the earth to be with God again, Jesus said this to his disciples:

"I am with you now. I will always be with you, wherever you go, until the end of the world." (Matthew 28.20)

The Ark

The ark is a symbol of rescue. Read the story of Noah on page 45 and find out why.

Sometimes the ark is used as a symbol of the Church. The Church is like a boat, an ark, sailing the waters of life. Noah was not alone in the ark, he had his family with him. In the same way the Christian family sails through life as a family. The journey may be rough at times, but they know they will be safe in the end.

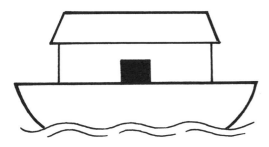

Activity

• Some churches have ceilings which look like upturned boats. The church itself is a gigantic boat symbol. The word "Nave", which is the body of the church, means "ship". Look in your local parish church and see if it has a wooden ceiling which looks like an upturned boat.

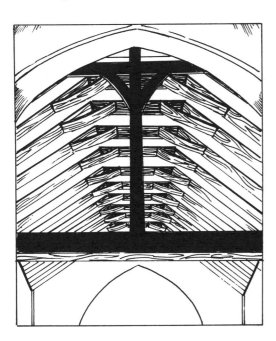

Rainbows of Promise

There are seven stories containing promises in this section. Find out the promise in each story or passage.

Activity

- Draw seven wide bands of colour in the shades of the rainbow. On each band, write one of these promises. Make sure you make your rainbow big enough to contain them.

Summer and winter...
You will have a son and one day this land will be yours.

- The Bow of War

    When you have finished, use a black crayon or felt pen to make the top of the rainbow like an archer's bow. The word "rainbow" in the Bible means "bow of war". The sign of the rainbow meant that God had put away his bow of war: he was no longer angry. The bow points away from the earth.

David is Chosen to be King

Read the story "David is Chosen to be King" on page 51.

Activity

• Make a simple outline of the boy David from A4 size sugar paper. Cut it out.

• Make a number of smaller "Davids", all the same shape but reducing in size. Each "David" shape should fit under a larger one without being seen.

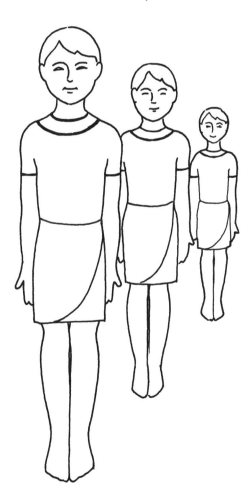

• Place all the "David" shapes on a plain piece of paper slightly larger than A4. Place them underneath each other so that only the largest shape can be seen.

• How could you fix them to the paper so that you could lift the larger shapes and see the smaller ones underneath?

Think about it

Do you tend to look at the outside of a person, or do you try to look at a person's inner qualities?

The Passover

Read the story called "Moses: Promises Start to Come True," on page 49.

During the Jewish celebration of Passover, ten drops of wine are spilt, one for each of the Ten Plagues.

Activity

• Draw ten drops down the side of your page and write beside each drop what each one of the plagues was. Look these up in a Bible; you will find them listed in the book of Exodus, chapters 7—11 (Good News Version).

• Read this poem and think about it carefully.

Seder
Why celebrate with bitter herbs,
salt tears of still–remembered slaves
and (though there's time now
for less hasty ways)
this joyless bread?

The salt reminds us still
of parting seas,
and, though there's time now,
once was none;
whilst plague took
Egypt's eldest sons
we brought to safety
our firstborn.

Pass over, Death;
Pass over, Death;
Passover…

Judith Nicholls
(*Dragonsfire,* Faber & Faber, 1990)

• Find out how Jews celebrate the events of this story, and the place this story
has in the Jewish faith.

CHANGE

Understanding the biblical ideas

The word change implies both continuity and alteration. This group of stories looks at the changes which took place in the lives of certain individuals and the role of God in those changes. It also looks at some people who changed on the inside.

Individuals such as Joseph and Jacob experienced tremendous changes in their circumstances. In the lives of Joseph and Jacob, God is seen as being in control of what was happening to them. The fact that Joesph was in the right place at the right time was no accident. Joseph was also eventually able to forgive his brothers and Jacob was reconciled to Esau, so relationships changed as well as events.

One of the Hebrew words for repentance means changing direction. It is as if someone was walking one way and then turned round and walked in the opposite direction. Paul changes from persecutor to Christian. Zacchaeus changes from thief to honest man. The concept of change on the inside is closely linked to forgiveness and rebuilding broken friendships. Forgiveness is useless without commitment to change. Saying sorry is not enough. Change is also part of the rebuilding involved in mending broken friendships.

John the Baptist called people to repent — to change. Baptism was an outward sign of an inward change. Jesus called people to repent because the Kingdom of God was close. He called them to change because God's rule was breaking into the world. The time had come for them to change and accept God as king. Repentance and change are integral to the Christian experience. No one can be a Christian and stay as they are. Christians believe that God changes people to be more like himself.

Introducing the passages

Talk about Transformers and other toys that change. With young children, use the dressing up box and let the children change their appearance on the outside. Investigate animals that change such as caterpillars. Talk about changing on the inside as Zacchaeus and Paul did.

With young people, read *Brown Ears: the adventures of a lost and found rabbit* (Lion, 1989) by S Lawhead. This is a lovely story of a lost "comfort" rabbit. Throughout all the changes in his life, God is with him, until, like Joseph, he ends up in the right place.

Talk about playing tricks. Perform some safe tricks suitable for the age group using a child's magic set. Read the story of Jacob.

Other useful passages

The other episodes of the Jacob story can be found in Book 1, pages 24–25, 53.

The other episodes of the Joseph story can be found on pages 6–7; Book 1, 46–47.

Ruth's life involves many changes: her story can be found in Book 1, pages 5, 21.

John the Baptist called people to change. This can be found under "Jesus is Baptized", Book 3, page 31.

Any of the healing miracles involves change. The following stories demonstrate that change: pages 32, 36, 103; Book 1, 8.

The change brought about by the Holy Spirit can be seen in the story "Dry Bones" in Book 3, page 94.

Cross–curricular links

English
- Write stories for younger children about change, for example: "The Ladybird who changed her spots!" (3)
- Tell the story of Zacchaeus using a simple storyboard. (1, 3)
- Find out the names of Joseph's ten older brothers. Choose one of those brothers. Write as if the brother is telling the story. Start your story: "I am Judah…" (Gad, Asher, etc.). How did the brother feel about Joseph? How did he feel after he had sold him? (2, 3)

Technology
- Look at toys which change, such as Transformers and Cinderella dolls (two–headed dolls which are reversible). Make a simple Topsy Turvy doll for a young child. This is a doll which has a sad face on one side and a happy face on the other. (1, 2)
- Look at technological changes in history, e.g. transport, household machinery.

History
- Sequence events in a story to show change. (1)
- Put artefacts in chronological order to demonstrate change; identify the difference between past and present, e.g. clothes, transport. Describe changes over a period of time. (1, 3)
- Look at different kinds of historical changes, e.g. rapid/gradual, local/national. (1)
- Investigate people who caused major change, e.g. Henry VIII (his role in the Reformation in England), Gutenberg and printing. Read accounts of the same events from different points of view and notice how perspective can change the content depending on who is writing. (1, 2, 3)

Science
- Changes in materials: stretching/squashing, heating/cooling. (1, 3)
- Changes in cooking: melting/freezing, dissolving/decay/waste/pollution. (2, 3)
- Changes in the weather: seasons/measuring weather/temperature. (1, 3)

Mathematics
- Change can be explored in various ways in maths. Money: giving change. (2)
- Making shapes and changing them using various forms of symmetry. (4)
- Changes in direction: angles and compasses. (4)
- Place value: changing the position of numbers. (2)

Art
- Changes of colour: mix primary and secondary colours. (1)
- Dyeing: use natural dyes such as onion skins. (1)
- Shape: exploded shape pictures. (1)

Music
- Changes in rhythm, pitch, timbre, etc. Create tone changes in self–built instruments by changing the shape, or the length of elastic bands, or the contents of shakers. (1)

Geography
- Changes in the local area: look at aerial pictures to detect changes. (1, 5)
- Changes in environment: give an account of a recent or proposed change in a locality, e.g. redevelopment or rain forest destruction. (4, 5)
- Changes in landscape affected by weathering. (3) (SAT 3)

Personal and Social Education
- Changes in attitude: tolerance/prejudice against people of other races or cultures. What can we do to effect change of attitudes? (EAT 1)
- Helping people to change. How can we help people to change unacceptable behaviour? Look at role modelling, sanctions and rewards. (EAT 1)

PE/Dance
- Explore changes in speed, level, shape and direction. (KS 1/2)
- Use changes in weather as a stimulus for movement: from storm to calm, from hot to cold. Represent by movement the changes which take place in people, e.g. growing old. Be careful about stereotyping in this. (KS 1/2)

ZACCHAEUS CHANGES
Luke 19.1–10 ▶ *page 63*

A Christian perspective
This is a story of a changed life. The evidence of that is Zacchaeus' changed behaviour. He stops being a thief and gives back four times as much as he stole, which was more than the compensation designated by law (except in certain cases). He also goes beyond the legal requirements in giving away half his goods. The internal change has an external outworking.

Points of interest

1. The law normally required the thief to pay back the amount stolen plus an extra one fifth.
2. As a tax collector, Zacchaeus would have been viewed as a collaborator with the Romans, as he collected taxes for them. Tax collectors also charged extra which they kept for themselves. Zacchaeus was a chief tax collector, responsible for a whole area.
3. Zacchaeus is isolated in his community. This must have made him fairly desperate, as he is prepared to make a fool of himself climbing a tree.
4. Jesus was frequently criticized for the company he kept. He mixed with "tax collectors and sinners". Jesus said he was like a doctor, he went where he was most needed.

PAUL MEETS JESUS
Acts 7.54—8.3; 9.1–31 ▶ *page 64*

A Christian perspective

The main point of this story for Christians is that Paul changed from being a persecutor of Christians into being a Christian himself. Christians believe this was the result of a dramatic experience on the Damascus Road when Paul "heard" Jesus. The Christian community was slow to accept Paul, which was hardly surprising. His own persecution and humiliating escape from Damascus in a basket helped his acceptance. In this story, Jesus identifies with the early believers, taking their ill–treatment as his own. He says the same in Matthew: "Whoever receives you, receives me."

Points of interest

1. Paul was a very well–educated Jew who had been to university. He studied under Gamaliel, a Jewish teacher who was tolerant towards Christians — an attitude which Paul does not seem to have taken on board. Paul was in a position of influence as he was trusted by the High Priest.
2. The early believers were largely Jewish. Damascus in Syria was outside the territory of Judaea, but all Jews were under the authority of the High Priests, no matter where they lived. This persecution caused many Christians to move to safer places, taking their faith with them. Persecution had its part to play in the spread of Christianity.
3. Paul was both a Jew and a Roman citizen. He would have spoken Aramaic, Hebrew, and Greek, and probably some Latin.

FROM JACOB TO ISRAEL
JACOB: EPISODE 2
Genesis 29—32.32 ▶ *page 66*

A Christian perspective

Jacob changed during his stay away from home. He left with only his wooden staff, escaping from his brother. He returns many years later a prosperous family man. In his flight and his wanderings, Jacob felt that God had been with him. Christians would see his meeting with God (an angel represented God) as a very important part of the story, for such meetings are rare in the Bible and often mark out someone as having a special job to do. Jacob had a trick played on him, similar to the one he had played on Isaac. No doubt this brought home to him what he had done. His name was changed from Jacob to Israel, a name he bequeathed to the nation.

Points of interest

1. Jacob worked instead of paying a brideprice. A woman was not sold as a slave into marriage: rather her family was compensated for the loss of a worker.
2. Jacob worked fourteen years for Rachel. She was the mother of Joseph and Benjamin, which explains why Joseph became a favourite son.
3. Brides were heavily veiled at the time and Jacob would not have seen Leah until it was too late. Leah had many sons. The sons of Jacob made up the twelve tribes of Israel.

JOSEPH: FROM FAVOURITE TO SLAVE
JOSEPH: EPISODE 1
Genesis 37 ▶ *page 67*

A Christian perspective

For Christians the story of Joseph is a story of God in control. Joseph's life looked like a disaster but when he was needed, Joseph was in the right place at the right time. Christians would see this as God's planning rather than an accident. Joseph may have had a special job to do in the future but when he was young he was a spoilt brat. Before Joseph could fulfil his special role, he had to change.

Points of interest

1. The family of Joseph was riven by jealousy. Joseph was one of the two sons of Rachel, Jacob's favourite wife (he had four). Rachel had died after giving birth to Joseph's brother, Benjamin.
2. Joseph was given a special coat. The Hebrew word used to describe this coat can be translated

as "long–sleeved" or "many coloured". It may
have been white as special clothes often were. If
it was long–sleeved, it would have made work
difficult, emphasizing that Joseph was special in
his father's eyes and did not have to do as much
work as his brothers. It was the type of coat
given to the first–born son, which may have
meant that Jacob was putting Joseph in place of
Reuben, the eldest. In light of this, it is surprising
that Reuben is so generous to Joseph.

3. If Joseph had been made the "first–born", he
   would have inherited twice as much as his
   brothers, and would have been head of the clan
   after the death of his father.

4. As one of the youngest, Joseph should have been
   low in status. To suggest to his elder brothers
   and parents that they would one day bow to
   him, would have been particularly insulting in
   Middle Eastern society, which respected older
   members of the family.

5. Joseph was sold for twenty pieces of silver, the
   price of a male slave. The price was previously
   ten to fifteen pieces. By Moses' time it was fixed
   at thirty pieces of silver, the price paid for Jesus.

6 The Ishmaelites or Midianites were nomads who
   traded camels throughout the Near East.

Zacchaeus Changes

Luke 19.1–10

Zacchaeus was not a popular man. His job was to collect tax–money from the people to pass on to the hated Romans who ruled them. He always took more money than he should, so that he could keep the extra for himself. In this way he became very rich, but he was not happy. The people, most of whom were very poor, did not like him because of his greed, so he was very lonely. No one ever wanted to visit him, and no one would dream of inviting him to their house.

One day, he overheard people telling each other that Jesus was coming to visit the town. He had heard of Jesus. People loved to listen to him because he was a very good teacher. They said that he was even able to make sick people better. Zacchaeus decided that he would like to see Jesus.

Crowds of people were standing along the sides of the street, all of them pushing and jostling each other to get a good view. Zacchaeus realized that he would not be able to see over people's heads. He was too short! He asked some people he knew to let him squeeze between them to the front, but they just laughed at him and wouldn't let him through. He heard someone shouting, "He's coming! Jesus is here! Look!" Then someone else pushed through the crowd shouting, "He's healed that blind man who begs for money outside the town. Jesus has made him able to see!"

"What am I going to do?" thought Zacchaeus. "I really want to see Jesus." Just then he had a brainwave. Of course, he could climb up that tree over there. Quickly he scrambled up the tree, hoping no one would see him and laugh at him. Now he had a perfect view. He held on tightly to the tree trunk and looked out over people's heads. He could see a man coming down the street, stopping to talk to one or two people, smiling at everyone. This must be Jesus. Everyone was crowding round him. They all wanted to meet him. Zacchaeus wanted to as well, but he kept very still. How the people would laugh at him if they realized where he was!

Jesus came nearer and nearer. He was right under the tree now. Suddenly he stopped. He looked up, right at Zacchaeus. Zacchaeus held his breath. What would Jesus say? Then he realized that Jesus was telling him to come down. "Zacchaeus," he said, "I want to come to your house. Come on."

"My house?" thought Zacchaeus. He couldn't believe it. He slid down the tree and began to lead Jesus to his house.

Zacchaeus was amazed — and so were the other people! "Zacchaeus is an awful man," they muttéred to each other. "He's a thief! Why does Jesus want to visit him, of all people?" They watched the two men walk off together.

"Why is he bothering with me?" thought Zacchaeus. "Perhaps he doesn't know how I've treated people. Perhaps he thinks I'm a good person." But soon, as Jesus talked to him, Zacchaeus realized that Jesus did know all about him and about the money he'd stolen. "But he still cares about me. He still wants to be with me!" Zacchaeus could hardly believe this. He began to think carefully. He saw how wrong he'd been in the past, and he was very sorry. He told Jesus that he wanted to put things right. "I'll give back four times as much money as I stole," he said "and half my wealth I will give to the poor. And I won't cheat anybody ever again."

Paul Meets Jesus

Acts 7.54—8.3; 9.1–31

Paul watched with satisfaction as Stephen died. "One less Christian to worry about," he thought. He was eager to get rid of as many of these people as he could. Paul had his spies out in Jerusalem: he knew where the Christians lived and where they met for worship. He organized raids of their homes, and many of them — men and women — were thrown into prison to await trials. He had to stop these people deceiving the Jews by their lies.

But, despite all his efforts, some Christians did get away from Jerusalem. They travelled to other cities and began to teach about Jesus there. Soon, new Christian groups began to grow in these other cities. Paul had heard about one in Damascus. He was furious: would the Christians ever realize they were beaten? He went to the High Priest and asked for special letters from him, allowing Paul to continue his work in Damascus. The High Priest was pleased to agree: he thought that Paul was a good man, sharing his own hatred and distrust of the Christians, believing, like him, that Jesus had been a fake.

So Paul set off leading his group out of the city. The ride was long and tiring in the heat, but eventually he saw the walls of Damascus ahead. And then, suddenly, everything changed for Paul. There was light, dazzlingly bright, all about him. He fell on to his knees — and heard a voice saying, "Paul, why are you treating me like this?" He was devastated: in his experience, things like this just could not happen.

"Lord, who are you?" he gasped.

The answer came, "I am Jesus, the one you are ill–treating. Why do you keep refusing to listen to me, Paul? You're making your own life very difficult. Get up now, and go into Damascus. I'll tell you there what you must do next."

The men with Paul watched him in amazement. As they helped him to his feet, they realized that he could not see anything. Carefully, they led him into Damascus and there he stayed. For three whole days he was blind, and unable to eat or drink. Desperately he tried to make sense of what had happened. At last, he admitted that he had met Jesus himself, and that everything the Christians had said about Jesus was true. Hesitantly, he began to pray, asking God to teach him more about Jesus, and to forgive him for all he had done to hurt the Christians.

While Paul prayed, alone and frightened, Jesus spoke to him in a vision. He told him that a man called Ananias would come to him soon and that God would use the man to heal Paul. But Ananias himself was not keen to do what Jesus asked.

"We've all heard about this man, Lord," he objected. "He has had many of your followers arrested in Jerusalem and he's come to Damascus to do the same here!"

Then Jesus explained to Ananias how he had changed Paul. "I have chosen him to tell people about me, here in Israel, and in other countries," he told him.

So, Ananias went to Paul. He put his hands on him, and said that Jesus was healing his eyes, and giving him the Holy Spirit. At once Paul could see. He was

RESOURCE BANK 2: CHANGE

baptized immediately, and began his new work of teaching people about Jesus. He went to all the synagogues in Damascus, preaching bravely in each one. The Jews were amazed — what had happened to the man? They had been expecting him to arrest the Christians, not to join them. They became so annoyed at the change in him that they posted men at each gate of the city, ready to kill him when he tried to leave. Paul's new friends, the Christians he had come to destroy, rescued him by letting him down in a basket from one of the windows set into the city wall.

Later, Paul travelled back to Jerusalem. There, some of the disciples were afraid to trust him. They thought he might be pretending to be a Christian, just to trick them into giving themselves away. Gradually, though, they realized that the change in Paul was genuine. Over the years, he became one of the most important leaders of the Church. He travelled great distances, often in great danger, to tell people about Jesus, and he wrote many very important teaching letters to the different groups of Christians — letters which we can still read today. What a change in the man who had watched Stephen die!

From Jacob to Israel

JACOB: EPISODE 2

Genesis 29—32.32

After his long journey, Jacob was pleased to arrive at his Uncle Laban's house. He soon settled in there, helping to look after Laban's animals. After a month, though, Laban told him that he couldn't let him work without wages any longer. Now, Jacob had fallen in love with Laban's younger daughter, Rachel. So he said, "I'll work for you for seven years in return for permission to marry Rachel." Laban agreed to this. The next seven years did not seem long to Jacob, because he was happy there, waiting for his marriage.

The day of the wedding arrived, and Jacob married his bride. But then he realized that he had been tricked! His bride was not Rachel, but Leah, Rachel's elder sister! Furious, he went to Laban.

"Now listen, Jacob," Laban said, trying to calm him down. "In this country, we do not allow younger daughters to marry before their elder sisters. But now you have married Leah, you can marry Rachel, too, as long as you agree to work for me for another seven years."

Jacob agreed to this: he had to, because he still wanted to marry Rachel. So, for another seven years, he worked hard for his uncle. During this time, he had several children. He began to feel that he should return home, but Laban was not keen to let him go. He knew that he himself had grown much richer since Jacob had been working for him.

Finally, they reached an agreement. Jacob was to take all the spotted goats and sheep out of Laban's herds and into his own. Laban tried again to trick his nephew. He quickly hid away all such animals. But God was with Jacob, and many of the kids and lambs born in the next years were spotted. So Jacob grew rich and Laban became jealous.

"It is time to return home," God told Jacob, and Jacob was pleased. He often thought about his brother now, and wondered how he was. Had he forgiven him, he wondered? So he and his family packed their belongings, gathered together all their animals, and set off on the long road home.

One night, as they were travelling, a stranger came to Jacob and wrestled with him. They wrestled and struggled all night. Jacob realized the stranger was one of God's angels, and he asked the stranger to bless him.

The man replied, "Your name will no longer be Jacob, for that means a deceiver. Your name now is Israel — for that means a person who struggles with God." Then he blessed him, and left.

RESOURCE BANK 2: CHANGE

Joseph: from Favourite to Slave

JOSEPH: EPISODE 1

Genesis 37

One of Joseph's brothers spotted him while he was still a long way off.

"Well, look there!" he said. "Here comes the famous dreamer! Dad has sent him to check if we're doing our job properly!"

"Well, he chose the right person to send, didn't he? Joseph's good at telling tales about us. He got us into real trouble last time, didn't he?"

None of them really liked Joseph. They knew that their father, Jacob, loved Joseph much more than he loved them, even though they, being older, did most of the work — such as now, miles away from home, out in the wilds looking after the animals.

"Look! He's wearing his special robe, his present from Dad," one of them sneered. "Fancy putting that on just to check up on us! He does enjoy rubbing it in, doesn't he?"

"I don't mind the robe," one of them commented. "It's too fancy for me anyway. No, it's his dreams that annoy me. You'd think he'd at least have the sense to keep quiet about them. Instead, he can't wait to describe them to us."

"Yes, I agree, all that talk about our sheaves of corn bowing down to his."

"And what about the eleven stars and the sun and moon bowing down to him? Not just us, his eleven brothers, but Mum and Dad as well! Does he really think these dreams mean we're going to bow down to him in the future?"

"Yes," one replied seriously. "I think he really does believe his dreams are true."

"Well," Reuben put in hastily, "Dad was annoyed with him, too, about that last dream, remember."

"Not surprisingly!" came the retort. "No father likes to be told that he's going to have to bow down to his own son! I don't think I can put up with Joseph for much longer!"

"Then don't!" one of them replied. "This is our chance. No one will see us: let's kill him. We can hide his body down a well, and say that wild animals have killed him. That'll stop his dreams!"

Reuben was horrified. He tried, desperately, to think of a way to save Joseph. If he could keep him alive, he could rescue him later secretly. Yes, that was it.

"No, wait!" he interrupted, as the other brothers began to plan the details. "We mustn't kill him. Let's just throw him down the well, and leave him there to take his chances — but we mustn't actually kill him."

They agreed to this: why bother killing him? He'd soon die from starvation. So, as soon as Joseph reached them, they seized him, tore off the hated robe, and threw him roughly into the dry well. Then they calmly sat down to eat.

During their meal, a long line of camels came into view, heading towards them. They belonged to a group of merchants taking spices down into Egypt. Watching them gave Judah an idea.

Joseph: from Favourite to Slave — continued

"Listen!" he said. "If we leave Joseph here, all we'll gain is an end to his boasting. Now, what about selling him to these merchants? They're always on the look–out for slaves to sell to the Egyptians."

So they sold their young brother for twenty pieces of silver, and watched with satisfaction as he was dragged off to slavery. Then they killed one of their goats, and soaked Joseph's robe in its blood. Back home, they showed this to Jacob, pretending to be upset.

"We found this: is it Joseph's?" they asked him sorrowfully.

Jacob was devastated. His favourite son, Joseph, was dead. "I will never get over this," he told them. "I will miss Joseph until the day of my own death. Poor Joseph!"

RESOURCE BANK 2: CHANGE

Word Exchange

Activity

- Look at the two words below.

Hate   Love

- Can you change the word Hate to Love in as few moves as possible?

  You can only change one letter at a time.

  You must make a recognized word each time.

  You must keep four letters.

  Example:

  HATE change the H for an L to make LATE
  LATE change the A for a U to make LUTE

- Can you think of another pair of words, containing the same number of letters, which you could change in as few moves as possible? Look through the stories in this section for ideas.

  Example: poor — rich

Think about it

Word exchange is just a game about changing. In reality, to change someone from hating to loving is very difficult.

Read the stories of Paul and Zacchaeus on pages 64 and 63.

What made these two people change?

Joseph

Read the story of Joseph. You will find the complete story on pages 6, 67, and Book 1, page 46.

Activity

- This story is told with lots of flashbacks. Read the story carefully and sort it out into a sequence of events following on from one another.

- Number the events and put them in the right order.

  Example:

  1. Joseph is his father's favourite.

  2. Joseph is given a special coat.

  3. Joseph has two dreams. One about sheaves of corn, one about the sun, stars and moon.

- What changes happened to Joseph in the course of his life?

Think about it

For many years, Joseph's life looked like a disaster. Out of that disaster great good came: he saved his family and the Egyptians from starvation. Joseph believed God was with him through all the changes in his life.

Looking for Evidence

If a crime has been committed, the police look for evidence. Imagine there has been a burglary at your school. What evidence would you look for? What would count as evidence?

Activity

Read the story of Paul on page 64.

- People were very suspicious of Paul after he became a Christian. They thought it was a trick, which is hardly surprising considering his previous behaviour. What evidence was there that Paul had changed?

- Read through the story carefully, looking for evidence.

Read the story of Zacchaeus on page 63.

- How did Zacchaeus change?

- The people of Jericho did not trust Zacchaeus. He had been a thief and a traitor. How did Zacchaeus convince them he had changed?

- Read through the story of Zacchaeus looking for evidence of change.

Think about it

When people become Christians they begin to change. The change happens on the inside first and is very difficult to detect. The inward change should, however, eventually result in an outward change, as it did in the case of Zacchaeus and Paul.

CHANGE

Guilty!

All Christians change, not just once but many times. For a Christian, life is a process of changing to be more like Jesus.

Activity

Imagine that being a Christian is a crime — as it has been in the past. Can you make up a courtroom scene in which a person is accused of being a Christian.

• What evidence would you look for to prove someone was a Christian? What evidence would you look for in their beliefs? What would you look for in their behaviour?

Things to think about:
— How many people do you need for the scene?
— Do you need a jury? Who is going to be the judge?
— How is the jury going to vote, as a group or is each person going to vote separately?
— Do you need any props?

• The lawyers will need time to put together their case. Ask local Christians to help you do this.

Think about it

People's beliefs affect their behaviour. How do your beliefs affect the way you behave?

FIRE

Understanding the biblical ideas

Fire in the Bible is often a symbol of God. Fire usually indicates God is present. When Moses meets God in the desert, it is at the burning bush. When he meets God on the mountain, fire and smoke are there. A pillar of fire and cloud accompanies the Israelites through the desert — God travels with them. God proves he is real by fire on Mount Carmel.

Both wind and fire indicate the presence of the Holy Spirit. When the Spirit comes in Acts 2, Luke describes "what seemed to be tongues of fire".

Fire is a symbol of suffering: the three friends enter the fiery furnace. God does not spare them the fire but he is in it with them. God is present in their suffering and danger.

God is sometimes seen as a metalworker. Precious metal has to be melted in the fire to get rid of the impurities. The fire softens it so that it can be worked into something beautiful. Christian experience shows that it is often in the difficult times that people grow and change.

Fire is a symbol of judgement: the two evil towns of Sodom and Gomorrah are destroyed by fire. Fire is a symbol of hell in the New Testament. Judgement by fire is not included here, as the symbol of fire as judgement can be difficult for young children. God as judge is dealt with in the following stories: "Titles of God", Book 3, page 83, "The Parable of the Sheep and the Goats", Book 3, page 18, and "Noah", page 45 .

Introducing the passages

Talk about the different functions of fire: fire that cleanses, fire that warms, fire that destroys.

Pasteurization and heat sterilization are examples of fire which cleanses. Take in pasteurized milk and yogurt. Investigate how heat kills germs which spoil food.

Suffering is sometimes described as a fiery ordeal, fire standing for all hurt. The story of "The Three Friends in the Fire" is an instance of fire as suffering.

Talk about symbols and introduce the children to basic signs and symbols such as road signs. Move on to more abstract symbols — hearts, political symbols, symbols of various organizations. Introduce them to religious symbols such as candles and crosses. In each of the stories, God is represented by fire but in each case it is a different side of his character which is uppermost. In the story of the burning bush it is the God who calls: a God who has heard his people's prayers and answers them. In the story "The Escape from Egypt" it is a God who guides in a pillar of cloud and fire. In the story of "Elijah and the Prophets of Baal," it is a God who actively demonstrates his presence and calls for a decision.

Other useful passages

The rest of the Moses story can be found in Book 1, pages 19–20, 23; Book 2, 21, 49; Book 3, 82.

"Elijah meets God", Book 3, page 80, could be used. In this story, God is not in the fire or the wind, the symbols of God often used in the Bible. In this case, God is in the still small voice. The rest of the Elijah story can be found in Book 1, page 64, and Book 2, pages 33, 79.

"The Holy Spirit Comes", Book 3, page 96. Both fire and wind represent God the Holy Spirit in this story.

"The Ten Commandments", page 21. When Moses meets God on the mountain, fire indicates the presence of God.

Cross–curricular links

English

- Look at the poem "Tyger, tyger burning bright" (W Blake, *The Oxford Library of English Poetry,* OUP). How was the tiger burning? (1, 2)
- Read Pepys' account of the Fire of London (Bell and Hyman). What would you save if there was a fire in your house? What is really important? (1, 2)
- Explore the different roles of fire through poetry. The CEM booklet *Fire* contains a number of these and can be obtained from CEM, Royal Buildings, Victoria Street, Derby. (2)
- Read the book *Ears and the Secret Song* by M Doney (Hodder, 1991). Look at the positive role of fire in this book. (1, 2)

Music

- Listen to Stravinsky's *Firebird,* Handel's "Firework" music, and Scriabin's *Prometheus.* (2)
- In a group compose and perform a piece of music which represents some of the qualities of fire, e.g. healing fire, destructive fire. (1)

Art

- Paint pictures in hot colours. Use "hot–coloured" tissue paper overlapped to make a fiery background. Add black silhouettes for a bonfire, forest fire, fire of London scene, etc. (1)
- Using "hot–coloured" cold dyes, create batik pictures of flames or the sun. Look at the work of famous artists for inspiration, e.g. Van Gogh's suns in paintings such as *The Sower,* or Turner's *Fire at Sea.* (1, 2)

Mathematics

- Make a Venn diagram to show things you would save from a fire: collect ideas and sort them into groups. Is there a common thread? (5)

PE/Dance

- Interpret in dance the following music: *The Ritual Firedance* by de Falla and Stravinsky's *Firebird.* Think about a fire being lit, flickering, and roaring. Create a dance routine incorporating movements for flames, smoke, etc. Re–create the story of the Phoenix in dance form. (KS 1/2)

Science

- Investigate the range of fuel used in the home. Make sure all tests are run safely, by trained personnel, with due regard to safety regulations. Children should not be encouraged to light/investigate fires. (1, 4)
- Investigate the positive role of heat in sterilization and pasteurization. (3)
- Look at the changes, temporary and permanent, which fire brings about, e.g. firing clay, cooking. (3)

History

- Explore how people made fire and turned it into a useful servant. (1, 2)
- Investigate famous fires in history — Pepys' diary, accounts of London during the Blitz, etc. (1, 2, 3)

Technology

- Design an effective fire warning sign. Look at shape, colour, lettering, etc. What makes a sign ineffective? (1, 2)

THE BURNING BUSH

MOSES: EPISODE 3

Exodus 3 ▶ *page 77*

A Christian perspective

The writer here emphasizes the "call" of Moses by God, God's presence being represented by the fire in the bush. Moses did not just decide to rescue his people. Like Gideon, Jeremiah, and Jonah, Moses was reluctant. Egypt might also have been a dangerous place for him still. Another important aspect is the compassion of God which caused him to rescue Israel and in doing this he kept a promise given earlier.

Points of interest

1. Moses takes off his shoes out of reverence because he is on holy (special) ground. Holiness is the quality which particularly characterizes

God in the Bible. The word "holy" means "separate from the realm of ordinary life", as well as morally holy.
2. Moses worked in the desert, probably to the south of Sinai, for many years as a shepherd. They were years of solitary preparation. Later, he was to return to this area to receive the Law.

THREE FRIENDS IN THE FIRE

Daniel 3 ▶ *page 78*

A Christian perspective

The friends in this story were prepared to stand up for their faith even if it meant dying. They were sure God could save, but knew that some people had died for their faith. Fire in this story, is the "fire" of suffering. In the fire there was a fourth figure, an angel who stood in the place of God. In this story, God did not save them from being thrown into the fire but he was in it with them.

Points of interest

1. Fire was used as a death penalty, among other methods. The Babylonians were noted for their cruelty.
2. Nebuchadnezzar set up a statue to be worshipped, probably one of a god. The ceremony described is probably the dedication ceremony. The three friends refused to take part because Jews were forbidden to worship idols.
3. The three friends and Daniel were originally deported to Babylon when the top people in Israel were creamed off by the Babylonians. By taking away any potential leaders, the Babylonians hoped to stop rebellion.

ELIJAH AND THE PROPHETS OF BAAL
ELIJAH: EPISODE 2
1 Kings 18 ▶ *page 79*

A Christian perspective

This is a story about making decisions. The Israelites were trying to worship two gods at once and Elijah tells them to make up their minds. Elijah wanted to prove to the Israelites that God was real and present. The sign of God's presence in this story is fire, as it was for Moses in the burning bush.

Prayer in the Bible never involves forcing God's hand. The prayers of the prophets of Baal and Elijah are different because of their beliefs. Prayer for the Israelites was part of a relationship. Elijah's prayer reflects this. It is not an attempt to manipulate God.

Points of interest

1. Ironically, Elijah's name means, "The Lord is God."
2. The sacrifice is, appropriately, part of the worship of God that should have been going on, but had lapsed. Even the altar needed repairing. Elijah pours precious water on the sacrifice.
3. Many Israelites had started worshipping both Baal (the Canaanite god) and Yahweh (the Israelite God), covering themselves just in case! Baal was seen as making the crops grow and making the earth fertile. It was difficult for the Israelites to ignore this faith, being farmers themselves.

THE ESCAPE FROM EGYPT
MOSES: EPISODE 5
Exodus 13.17–22 ▶ *page 81*

A Christian perspective

The Exodus is a story of God rescuing his people from a situation which looked impossible. The writer also emphasizes God keeping his promise. God is pictured with his people when they face a new and difficult situation: the image used is that of a cloud. It is a "bright cloud" which, like the fire, represents God. It is God himself shepherding his people out of Egypt.

Points of interest

1. The Red Sea may be a mistranslation for the Reed Sea, part of the Bitter Lake area, where the Suez Canal is today. The Israelites would have gone about ten or fifteen miles, which would be a reasonable journey with animals and children.
2. The Egyptians had a good chariot force. Pharaoh himself fought from a chariot which would have been useless in the marsh left behind after the water had retreated.
3. The bread eaten at Passover today is still unleavened — made without yeast — in memory of the rush to leave Egypt.

The Burning Bush

MOSES: EPISODE 3

Exodus 3

Moses shaded his eyes and took one last look at the landscape. He had worked as a shepherd in the desert south of Sinai for many years. Now he was leaving. He lifted up his son to his wife, and she settled the child in front of her. He patted the donkey, and led it down the track. It seemed a long time since he had left Egypt, but now at last he was on his way home.

Just a few days ago, he had been busy at work as usual, looking after his father–in–law's sheep. He had led them through the desert and on to the lower slopes of Mount Horeb, hoping to find some fresh grass for them. He'd found something else instead, something very strange. He saw a bush which was on fire. That in itself wasn't strange: the hot sun did sometimes cause fires in that dry area. But then he had realized that this was no ordinary fire. The bush itself was not burning! Its leaves were still green, and its branches weren't charred or even scorched! The fire was still there, though. He could see its bright flames clearly. He had moved closer to the bush — and then someone had called him by name. "I'm here," answered Moses — and then he heard God speaking to him.

"Don't come any closer! This is a special place: take off your sandals. I am the God of your people." Moses had been afraid but God had carried on. "I have seen how my people suffer in Egypt. I am going to rescue them and give them a new rich country. I am sending you to bring them out of Egypt."

Moses was dismayed! "I can't do that!" he answered. "I'm not powerful! What if they don't believe me? I can't even speak well. It's just impossible." But God had answered all his objections.

"I am the Lord. You will tell your people that I have sent you. I will tell you what to say and your brother Aaron will help you too. I will give you the power to do wonderful things so that the people and Pharaoh will see that you are my servant." Since that strange meeting, Moses had packed up his belongings, prepared his family for the journey and said goodbye to his father–in–law. Now he was reluctantly on the road, heading back to Egypt.

Suddenly he realized someone was coming. He watched the man carefully. It was his brother Aaron! God had promised that Aaron would meet him on the road — and here he was! The two brothers were pleased to see each other after so long apart. "Why are you returning to Egypt?" Aaron queried. So Moses explained everything that had happened.

Back in Egypt, the two brothers called together all the leaders of the Hebrew slaves. "God is going to rescue us. He has a new country for us, where we will be free and have all we need." When they heard this, the people thanked God for hearing their prayers, and for sending Moses and Aaron to lead them.

Three Friends in the Fire

Daniel 3

The people stood on the plain before the great golden statue. When they heard the music begin, they fell to their knees and worshipped. They did not dare to do otherwise. The king had said that anyone who refused to worship his new statue would be thrown into a blazing furnace. No wonder the people did as they were told!

But three young men did dare to disobey. Some of Nebuchadnezzar's officials hurried to tell him the bad news. "O king," they said, "three men have dared to disobey you. Abednego, Shadrach and Meshach have not worshipped your statue. In fact, they do not worship any of your gods."

The king was furious. "Bring them to me!" he shouted. "Let's see what they have to say for themselves."

The three men were brought in. The king decided to be merciful. After all, they had always worked well for him. "Is it true that you have not worshipped my statue?" he asked. "I'll give you one more chance. If you bow down and worship it next time, well, we'll forget the whole thing. If you don't, though, you will be thrown into the furnace. I'd like to see your god get you out of that !" he ended, laughing scornfully.

Abednego, Meshach, and Shadrach answered the king calmly: "We do not need to argue with you, Nebuchadnezzar. We will never worship your gods or your golden statue. Throw us into the furnace! If our God wishes to rescue us, he will do so — with no trouble at all. But even if he doesn't rescue us, we will still never worship any other god."

Now Nebuchadnezzar was even more furious. How dare they! "Make the furnace seven times hotter than usual! Tie them up and throw them in!" he ordered.

By the time the three men were thrown into the furnace, the fire was so fierce and hot that some of the soldiers were killed by the heat when they just got near to the entrance. But Nebuchadnezzar leapt to his feet amazed. "Look!" he shouted. "We put three men in, didn't we? Look now! I can see four figures there, walking round. They're not hurt. They're not even still tied up. One of them looks like a god, not a man." He walked over towards the furnace. "Meshach! Shadrach! Abednego!" he shouted. "Come out, servants of God."

And they came out. Nebuchadnezzar peered into the furnace: there was no one else there now! The three were immediately surrounded by the puzzled officials. They had not been burned at all. Their clothes were not even scorched! Their hair and their clothes did not even smell of fire or smoke.

Then Nebuchadnezzar praised God. "God sent an angel to look after these three, because they trusted in him, and would have died rather than disobey him," he told his people.

RESOURCE BANK 2: FIRE

Elijah and the Prophets of Baal

ELIJAH: EPISODE 2

1 Kings 18

For three years Elijah had hidden from the king. Many people had been sent to find him, but God had kept him safe. In all that time, no rain had fallen on the parched ground. Now God had told him it was time to go to King Ahab. God was going to prove to the king and to the people that he was the true God of Israel. So here was Elijah, in front of the king — Ahab was not pleased to see him!

"Is it really you, trouble maker?" he shouted at him.

"Yes," answered Elijah. "But it isn't me who has done all this. You're the one who has caused Israel all this trouble, you and that evil wife of yours, Jezebel. None of this would have happened if she hadn't brought with her all those prophets of Baal and tried to stamp out worship of the true God. But now, I propose a contest; order all the people to come to Mount Carmel. Gather together all the prophets who serve Baal, and we will see who is the true God of Israel."

So all the people gathered on the Mount. They were all wondering what was going to happen. Elijah stood alone and defiant. He had been right about the rain. He had predicted the drought. Was it possible that he was right about God and Baal too? But then, it was dangerous to say you followed God. Queen Jezebel had had no end of people killed for saying that! There were four hundred and fifty prophets of Baal but Elijah stood alone. Surely he would lose any struggle here today!

Elijah turned and spoke to the people. "How long are you going to dither about? If you believe the Lord is your God, follow him. If you believe Baal is, follow him. Decide!" No one answered — what should they say? "Listen!" shouted Elijah. "I am the only prophet of the Lord here. You can see Baal has four hundred and fifty prophets. Right. Fetch two bulls for us. Baal's prophets can choose one, kill it and prepare it as a sacrifice for their god. I will do the same with the other bull. But we won't set fire to the wood. We'll ask our gods to do that — and we'll see what happens. The god who sends fire to burn the sacrifice will have shown us that he is the real God."

"Yes, that's a good idea! We'll do that!" the people answered.

So Baal's prophets prepared the sacrifice, put it on his altar and began to pray. They prayed and prayed and shouted to Baal — and nothing happened. After several hours of this, Elijah began to mock them. "Come on, try harder. Perhaps your great god is asleep or on a journey, or busy elsewhere. He can't hear you. You'll have to pray even more loudly." So the prophets tried harder. For hours they shouted and pleaded and begged. But no fire came.

Then Elijah stepped forward. He rebuilt the stone altar of the Lord which had been left to collapse. Then he ordered the servants to dig a deep trench around the altar and to pour gallons of water over the altar and the meat which lay upon it! Again and again they soaked the sacrifice until the water had run off the altar, over the ground and filled the trench. Then he prayed. "O Lord, the God of our fathers, show us all today that you are God in Israel, and that I am your obedient servant. Answer my prayer, Lord. Let these people know that you are God."

Then fire fell. It fell on the altar and burned the sacrifice. It fell on the wood and the stones of the altar, and burned them. It burned the soil around the altar, and it even dried up the water in the trench.

And the people shouted, "Yes ! The Lord is our God, the God of Israel."

The Escape from Egypt

MOSES: EPISODE 5

Exodus 13.17–22

What a commotion! What a rush! The Hebrew slaves were leaving Egypt at last. They quickly bundled up their things. They gathered together their animals. They loaded up their carts and themselves. There wasn't even time to wait for the bread to rise! "Don't put in the yeast. There's no time! We'll have to cook it as it is!" Everyone was hurrying and rejoicing. "We're leaving! God has kept his promise. We're free!"

Soon they were ready, and the long line of people and animals began to move. They were leaving! They walked out of Egypt, out into the desert. God guided them. During the day, they could see a great pillar of cloud moving ahead of them. At night, a pillar of fire gave them light. If they had to move at night, they could follow this. They walked on and on. They were going to their new land!

When all the Hebrew slaves had left, Pharaoh suddenly realized that he had lost all his workers! "What have we done?" he shouted, forgetting all the troubles his people had suffered. "Fetch them back! Send the army." And the great Egyptian army, with its powerful, fast chariots, rushed out after Moses and his people.

When the people saw the great cloud of dust and heard the thunder of hooves, they knew at once what was happening. They were terrified! They were trapped between the Red Sea and the Egyptian army! "What have you done to us?" they shouted at Moses. "It would have been easier for us to carry on as slaves than to die out here in the desert!"

But Moses spoke calmly to them. "Don't be frightened. God knows what he is doing. Just wait patiently." Then God told him to hold out his staff over the sea. A great wind sprang up and the water of the sea was driven back. All night the wind blew and the water was rolled back to leave its bed dry. And all night the pillar of cloud stayed in between the Hebrews and the Egyptians, stopping the Egyptians from attacking the Hebrews. So Moses led the people across the sea — on dry land. But when the Egyptians tried to follow, the water rushed back, and they were drowned.

Elijah and the Prophets of Baal

Read the story of "Elijah and the Prophets of Baal" on page 79.

When Elijah challenged the prophets of Baal to a contest, he was trying to get the people of Israel to make up their minds concerning whom they wanted to worship.

He told them off for not making up their minds. They were like people standing at a fork in the road unable to make up their minds which way to go. When people behave like this, we sometimes say they are "sitting on the fence".

This story has been translated into various languages. In each case, the translators asked the people how they would describe the Israelites' behaviour. When Christians of Bengal were asked how they would translate this saying, they said:

"How long will you remain with your feet in two boats?"

This is because the people of this region are always coming and going in long shallow boats. Imagine having your feet in separate boats. What would happen? Is this a good way of describing what the Israelites were doing?

Activity

• Make up your own saying that will express the Israelites' behaviour, or try to capture their behaviour in a cartoon.

Think about it

Do you sometimes have difficulty in making up your mind?

The Burning Bush

Read the story of Moses and "The Burning Bush" on page 77.

Group activity

- As a group, make a collection of fire words.

- Cut a number of small flame shapes from scraps of paper. Use colours suitable for fire. Write your flame words on the scraps of paper.

- Plant some twigs in a pot of damp sand. (Only use twigs cut in pruning from safe plants.) Hang your flame words from the branches.

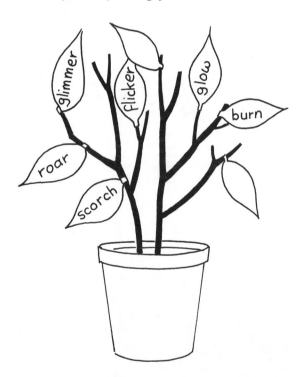

- Look at this poem on the burning bush.

  Moses smelt the crusty smell of smoke,
  He saw before him, lighting up his face, a burning bush.
  He felt the smooth wet rock.
  The taste of sourness and sweat was in his mouth,
  He heard the sweet, soft voice of God.

- Using some of the words from your "bush of flames", write your own poem, or piece of descriptive writing, about the burning bush.

Leading and Guiding

Read the story "The Escape from Egypt" on page 81.

In the story, the Israelites were led through the desert by a pillar of fire and a pillar of cloud. God guided them through an unknown place with a sign they could see.

 *Group activity*

- Look at the maze below. Write a set of instructions to a friend to help them to find their way through the maze.

- When you have finished your instructions, give them to a friend to test out.

Think about it

- Life sometimes looks like a maze, and many people feel that they need someone to guide them through it. Christians do not have a pillar of fire to show them the way through life, as the Israelites had a pillar of flame to guide them through the wilderness.

- Ask local Christians how they think God guides people today.

The Flame of Suffering

Read the story called "Three Friends in the Fire" on page 78.

The three friends in this story faced being thrown into the fire. In this case, they were saved but that is not always so: many people do suffer for their beliefs. Fire stands for all suffering, whether that suffering is being thrown into the fire, as the three friends were, or whether it is suffering of a different sort. The suffering of poverty, persecution, disaster, and illness can all be summed up in the term "fiery", because they all hurt in some way, just as burns hurt.

Activity

• Make a series of large flames. How could you do this?

• On the flames, write some of the things which cause suffering in the world: famine, drought, etc. If you want some help with ideas write to some of the relief agencies for information.

Useful addresses

Action Aid, Hamlyn House, Archway, London N19 5PG
Christian Aid, P.O. Box 100, London SE1 7RT
Cafod, 2 Romero Close, Stockwell Road, London SW9 9TY
Tear Fund, 100 Church Road, Teddington, Middlesex TW11 8QR
Oxfam, 274 Banbury Road, Oxford OX2 7DZ

Think about it

God rescued the three friends. God also works through people. Do we also have a part to play in rescuing people from the fire of suffering?

PEACE

Understanding the biblical ideas

Christians believe that God's intention in creation was to make a world which was harmonious and peaceful, but evil has caused disharmony. Yet God gave people a vision of peace, an echo from that first peace. The Bible contains many passages that hope for peace, for the Israelites often experienced war and famine, poverty and oppression. The Bible ends with a vision of peace, a re-creation, a world where peace is restored.

The hope for peace is related to the hope for the Messiah. One day, God's special king will come and restore lost peace. In the New Testament the angel's message at Jesus' birth was, "Peace on earth". Christians believe Jesus came to make peace between God and humanity, to rebuild the broken relationship. This is the heart of the concept of peace — the harmony between God and his people.

Jesus showed his power to bring peace in the middle of a storm on Lake Galilee. Christians also believe Jesus brings a deep personal peace, often in the midst of the stormy circumstances of life.

The Hebrew word *shalom* describes a positive concept of peace. It is right relationships, wholeness and well being. It is the ending of war, but it is more than all this. Peace is when wrong and the results of wrong are put right.

The dove and an olive branch are both from the story of Noah. The dove was released by Noah and it brought back an olive branch. The flood was over, peace was restored. Both have become symbols of peace. Throughout the Bible, there is a vision of peace. Sometimes, in the Old Testament, this vision is held in tension with an acceptance of war. There was a belief that one day true peace would come: fighting would cease and swords would be beaten into ploughshares.

Introducing the passages

Discuss situations the children find peaceful, and ones they find lacking in peace. What creates a peaceful situation?

Explore things which rob people of their peace: worry, busy–ness, fear, illness, etc. This needs handling very sensitively. Children need to be given practical strategies for handling worry, etc. The session needs to end on a very positive note.

Read the stories of Jesus' healing and how he created peace that way.

Look at newspapers and see how peaceful or lacking in peace the stories are. Select papers carefully. Ask the children to examine how peaceful their community is. Sometimes our lives are relatively peaceful, though the news is full of war. Why doesn't peace make the news?

Create a positive peace display made up of good, peaceful, news. Biblical sayings on peace can be added from the passage entitled "Visions of Peace", page 94.

Talk about "disturbing the peace" and what is meant by that term. Read the story of Elisha.

Other useful passages

"Noah", page 45.

The fruits of the Spirit include peace. See under the title "Understanding the Holy Spirit", Book 3, page 97.

The section on "Rescuers", Book 1, pages 109–115. These are people who restored peace.

The healing miracles which were part of Jesus' mission of bringing peace to a troubled world, pages 32, 36; Book 1, 8.

Jesus' message of peace, pages 19; Book 1, 83.

Cross–curricular links

English

- Discuss the ideas behind: "peace", being "at peace", and "peace and quiet". (1)
- Create cartoons with the caption: "Peace is ..." (2)
- Read extracts of *Charlotte's Web* (E B White, Hamish Hamilton, 1952; Penguin, 1969). What gave Charlotte peace of mind? What about Wilbur? (1, 2)
- Use reference books to find out information about famous peace makers in history: Desmund Tutu, Mahatma Ghandi, the King family (Martin Luther King's family still work for peace). (2)
- Write a poem about peace. It could be a Haiku poem (3 lines with 5, 7, 5 syllables respectively). (3)
- Look at the different types of peace/lack of peace in Ted Hughes' *The Iron Man* (Faber, 1985). (1, 2)

Art

- Paint pictures to depict moods of quiet/disquiet. (1)
- Paint abstract designs for sounds or feelings of strife and peace. (Use Holst's music *The Planets* for stimulus.) (1) (Mu 2)

Mathematics

- Look at the symbol of peace, the dove, and create tessellating patterns after the style of Escher. (4)
- Use the symbol of the dove to create geometrical patterns using reflective, rotational, and translational symmetry. (4)
- Using LOGO, generate graphics to represent symmetrical doves. (5)

Music

- Use any available instruments to depict moods of quiet/disquiet, peace/discord. Link this with art. (1)

- Listen to Holst's *The Planets* — Mars the bringer of war and Venus the bringer of peace. What differences in tempo, etc. are there? (2)
- Explore some of the peace "protest" songs such as "Last night I had the strangest dream". (Kensington Music Ltd., *Alleluya,* A&C Black, 1980) and "The answer is blowing in the wind". (2)

Technology

- Design and make a collage depicting Christian peace as a fabric collage or piece of embroidery. Mount or frame it appropriately. Evaluate and improve upon your original design. (1, 2)

PE/Dance

- Explore peaceful and angry movements in dance. Use Holst's music *The Planets,* (Mars the bringer of war and Venus the bringer of peace), as stimulus. What differences in tempo, etc. can be heard? (KS 1/2)

Personal and Social Education

- What brings peace in relationships? Is conflict always wrong? (EAT 1)
- Write some advice on peaceful friendships. Books such as *Coping with Conflict* by F M Nicholas (LDA, 1987) and *Co-operate* by the Peace Education Project (6 Endsleigh St., London, WC1 0DX may be helpful. (EAT 3)

History

- Explore how the *Pax Romana* helped in the spread of Christianity. (1, 3)
- Using the unit, "Britain since 1930", look at the impact of war (lack of peace) on society. (1, 2, 3)

ELISHA AND THE SYRIANS
2 Kings 6.8–23 ▶ *page 91*

A Christian perspective

This story depicts God fighting for Elisha; the chariots of fire are symbolic of the forces of God. Christians believe that God is active in the world as this story portrays. Elisha has to disturb the Syrians' peace by asking God to take away their sight in order to bring a deeper peace. There is a tension in the Old Testament between the ideal of peace and an acceptance of war. It is a tension many Christians feel.

Points of interest

1. The captives are treated as honoured guests instead of prisoners of war.

2. The Syrians were the enemies of Israel. There were frequent wars and raids.
3. Israel by this time had split into two kingdoms. The northern kingdom was called Israel, the southern was called Judah. The capital of the northern kingdom was Samaria.

CALMING THE STORM
Mark 4.35–41 ▶ *page 92*

A Christian perspective

This story is important for Christians because it demonstrates Jesus' power over nature. As with most miracles, for Christians it points to who Jesus is. He brings calm to an angry sea just as he can bring peace to troubled minds and bodies, and peace in relationships. Like most of Jesus' miracles Christians believe it points to who he is. The story is like that of Jonah in which God is in command of the storm. Please see the note in Book 1, page 92.

Points of interest
1. Jesus' disciples were experienced fishermen but sudden storms happen on the Sea of Galilee. The sea is very low and is encircled by hills — the name "Galilee" means circle. The wind funnels down the valleys and hits the sea, causing sudden storms.
2. The stern of the boat had a small seat. This is where Jesus lay. It was the place of honour.
3. "Peace, be still," is literally, "Be muzzled".

CREATION SPOILT
Genesis 3 ▶ *page 93*

A Christian perspective
However the story is interpreted, the writer emphasizes that this world is now not as good as it was when God created it. The good world that God created was spoilt by human disobedience. It is a story of evil creeping into a good world, spoiling a close relationship with God. It is the story of shattered peace. Fear, deception, and guilt entered a world that had known none of them. Christians believe that the wrong and sorrow that mar our world were not intended by God. Peace was broken in the infant world. Relationships were severed and life became hard. Christians believe it was in order to restore that lost peace that Jesus came.

Points of interest
1. The serpent is seen as the agent and a symbol of evil, not the source of evil itself.
2. "Eden", the name of the garden, became a symbol of all that is good. Christian hope looks forward to a time when relationships will be restored to that original closeness or even closer, a time when all sorrow and wrong will cease. The last book in the Bible contains a vision of that restored peace (Revelation 21).

VISIONS OF PEACE
Isaiah 2.4; 11.6–9; Luke 2.14; Matthew 5.9; John 16.33; Ephesians 2.14–15; 6.15; Romans 12.18; Revelation 21.3–5 ▶ *page 94*

A Christian perspective
In the Bible, peace is not a negative calm. The Hebrew word "peace" is "shalom" which is very positive. Christians believe Jesus can give an inner peace, a peace which trouble and hardship cannot destroy. Such peace is like the sea which may be stormy on the surface but has calm water deep underneath. Peace is also a physical thing. It is having a whole body and mind. The healing miracles, in which both body and mind were healed, were part of Jesus' role as a peace–bringer. Peace is when a land is ruled with justice and love — a land where war is banished. Peace can also be found in relationships. The angels announce peace at the birth of Jesus. The Bible describes Jesus as the one who brings people peace with God and others. Peace is both a hope for the future and a present reality. There is a pragmatic recognition that peace in this world, human peace, is a fragile affair. True, long–lasting peace will not come until the end of time. In Revelation, John writes of the final peace when the world is made new — a new Eden.

Points of interest
1. The ideal of peace is always held in tension with an acceptance of war in the Old Testament.
2. The passages from the Old Testament were spoken to specific situations, when the nation was threatened with war. A Christian reading those passages would accept that they were spoken to a specific historical situation, but also hold that they have a long–term significance as well.

Elisha and the Syrians

2 Kings 6.8–23

The King of Syria could not understand it. "Every time I prepare for battle or set up an ambush for the Israelites, they already know about it, and avoid it. There must be a traitor among you. Who is working for my enemy, the King of Israel?"

His officers looked at each other. They knew it wasn't one of them. "There is no traitor here, my lord the king," one officer said. It's that prophet — Elisha — in Israel. He knows everything about you and your plans. It's he who keeps warning the King of Israel."

The king was furious. "Then we must capture him!" he shouted, and he sent a powerful army into Israel to find the prophet.

Elisha was staying in a city called Dothan. One morning his servant had a terrible shock when he got out of bed. He had gone, yawning, to open the shutters. Looking out, he saw an army! He rushed over to Elisha. "My Lord," he gasped, "the whole city is surrounded by chariots and soldiers. What can we do?"

But Elisha seemed quite calm. "Don't be frightened," he said. There are many more fighters on our side than on the enemy's!"

The servant was amazed. What did Elisha mean? Where was their army? He looked out of the windows. "There aren't any on our side!" he thought.

Elisha was watching him. He knew what he was thinking. He prayed, "God, let my servant see who is really out there."

Just for a moment, the servant could see hundreds of chariots, bright with fire, all around the city. He realized that this was God's army, come to defend them.

Elisha went out to face the enemy. As some of them rushed up to seize him, he asked God to close their eyes for a while so they couldn't see. Confused and lost, they staggered round. "I'll help you," Elisha said. "You've come to the wrong place. I'll guide you to where you should be."

The prophet led them to the city of Samaria, where the King of Israel was staying. There he asked God to let them see again. When they realized where they were, they were terrified! Israel's king would surely have them killed! But Elisha — the man they had come to capture — told his king to have food prepared for them! Then, when they had eaten it, they were to return to their own country. The Syrians could hardly believe it. When he heard all that had happened, the King of Syria gave up even trying to attack Israel, and the two countries were at peace with each other for many years.

Calming the Storm

Mark 4.35–41

Disciple speaking: Yesterday evening, Jesus asked us to sail over to the other side of the lake with him. We do this when we can. Jesus likes to get away from the crowds sometimes to pray by himself, or to spend some time teaching just us, his disciples. So we climbed into a fishing boat and set off. Jesus, as usual, had been busy all day and he was soon fast asleep. Two of the fishermen rowed, and the rest of us just rested, enjoying the quiet.

Then a storm hit us. You know how sudden they are on this lake. There's no warning: all is peaceful, and then the wind rocks the boat and the waves crash over you. Now, we're all used to these storms — the fishermen among us especially. But this one had us worried. We tried to control the boat, but the wind was so strong, that we all panicked. And Jesus was still asleep! Some of us struggled to wake him. "How can you sleep, Jesus?" someone shouted. "Don't you care about us? We're nearly drowning!"

Jesus woke up quickly then! He stood up and shouted, "Peace, be still!" at the water and the wind, telling them to calm down. And they did! We could tell the difference immediately. The wind dropped and the sea was calm and smooth again. Our boat just bobbed up and down gently. We all turned to look at Jesus "Don't you have any faith in me?" he asked. "Why were you so frightened?" Then he settled down again.

We didn't know what to think. "Who is he?" we whispered to each other. "Even the water and the wind do as he tells them. Who is this man we are following?"

Creation Spoilt

Genesis 3

God created a beautiful garden where Adam and Eve could live in peace and tranquillity. He chose only the most beautiful plants and trees to grow there and those with the most delicious fruit. But in the middle of the garden grew a special tree. "You can eat the fruit of any tree here except this one," God told Adam. "This one is special to me, do not touch its fruit." Adam was happy to obey God in this: after all, the garden was filled with many other beautiful fruits to eat.

Life was very happy and peaceful in the garden. He and Eve had all they needed and they were surrounded by beautiful plants and creatures. Adam and Eve were very happy: they had each other, and God was their friend.

Now, of all the animals God had created, one — the snake — was much more cunning than any other. He decided not to obey God, and to try to trick the humans into disobedience too.

One day, he sidled up to Eve. "Tell me," he began, "is it really true that God has forbidden you to eat any of the lovely fruit in this garden?" (He knew that this was not true, but he wanted to trick Eve.)

"No, that's not right," Eve answered. "We can eat fruit from any tree except for one — the tree in the middle of the garden."

"What rubbish! Fancy forbidding you to eat it! God knows that if you do eat it, you will immediately become as wise as he is — that's why you're not supposed to touch it!"

Eve went over to the tree, and looked at the fruit. She plucked a fruit off the tree: it certainly looked and smelt good. "If it's just going to make us wiser, I don't see why we can't eat it," she said to herself — and she bit deeply into the sweet–smelling, juicy fruit. Then she handed it over to Adam, and he ate too.

Then they realized they had done wrong. They were very ashamed. When they heard God calling them, they hid themselves away, unable to face him. But God knew where they were, and he knew what they had done.

"Why are you hiding?" he asked them. "Have you eaten some fruit from that tree?"

Adam was horrified. What should he say? He'd only eaten it to please Eve, hadn't he? Or had he? Hadn't he wanted to be wise too? Anyway, it was Eve who had actually given it to him. "Eve — the woman you made — she gave me the fruit!" he said hastily.

So God turned to Eve. "What have you done?" he asked sadly.

"It wasn't me!" Eve said quickly. "The snake made me eat it — he tricked me!"

God was very unhappy. Adam and Eve, whom he had made, and whom he loved, had disobeyed his one command — and now neither of them would even admit they had done wrong. He sighed deeply. So soon after he had made it, the peace of his beautiful world had been shattered.

"You must leave my beautiful garden," he said. "This wrong thing you have done has come between you and me. You must go out from here and live in another place. But out there life will not be as easy for you." Sadly, God took them out of his special garden, and they walked out into the countryside.

Visions of Peace

Isaiah 2.4; 11.6–9; Luke 2.14; Matthew 5.9; John 16.33;
Ephesians 2.14–15; 6.15; Romans 12.18; Revelation 21.3–5

God himself will end all wars and arguments between countries. So the people will make their swords into plough blades, and their spears into gardening tools. They will not need weapons any longer, for one nation will not attack another, and no one will be trained as a soldier. (Isaiah 2.4)

When the special king rules the earth, peace will come: "The wolf will live with the lamb, and the leopard and the goat will lie down and rest together. The calf and the lion will live with each other. Even a small child will be able to lead them around. The cow will graze alongside the bear, and their young will sleep together. The lion will share the ox's hay. A toddler will be safe playing near the hole of a once poisonous snake, and even if he puts his hand inside such a snake's nest, he will not be hurt. No one will be injured or killed in my Kingdom then, for knowledge about me and my love will fill everyone all over the world, just as the water fills the great hollows of the oceans." (Isaiah 11.6–9)

Glory to God in the highest heaven, and peace on earth, to those with whom he is pleased. (Luke 2.14)

Blessed are the peacemakers — they shall be called the sons of God.
(Matthew 5.9)

I have told you many things, my friend, so that you may have peace, even if your life is full of trouble and hardship. (John 16.33)

He [Jesus] is our peace. He has brought together as friends we who once were enemies. (Ephesians 2.14)

As far as possible, live at peace with everybody. (Romans 12.18)

Put on your feet the Good News of the gospel of peace. (Ephesians 6.15)

God's home will be with his people. They will be his people, and he will be their God. He will wipe away every tear from their eyes. For there will be no crying and no pain. For all of these things belonged to the world as it used to be. They will all disappear when the world is made new. (Revelation 21.3–5)

RESOURCE BANK 2: PEACE

Spears to Pruning Hooks

Read page 94. The Bible says that one day, weapons of war will be turned into gardening tools: spears will be hammered into pruning hooks.

Activity

Look at the spear and the pruning hook drawn below.
In six or eight moves change a spear to a pruning hook, only making a small change each time.
Example:

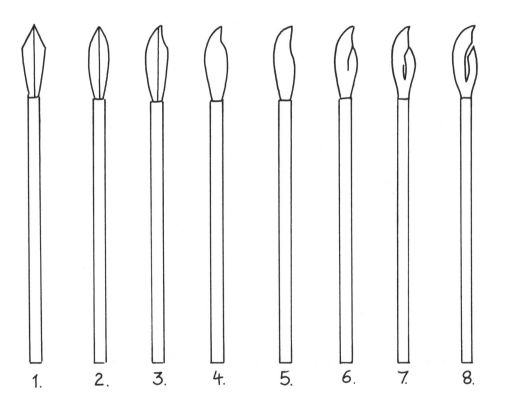

Think about it

In some countries today, tanks are being turned into tractors and guns into gardening tools, but there are still many weapons in the world. The Bible's dream of peace for this world remains a dream for the future, but Christians believe it is a sure hope because it depends on God.

Calming the Storm

Read the story called "Calming the Storm", page 92.

Try to capture the fierce storm and the quiet calm in a picture.

Activity

- Take a sheet of paper. Mix colours you think would be right for a stormy sea, mix them with plenty of water so that they are fairly runny. Using these colours paint the background for the stormy sea.

- When this is dry, use a thin brush to write words as wild waves and stormy seas. Use words that will describe a wild sea and how the disciples were feeling.

- Take another sheet of paper. Mix colours for a calm sea, making them quite runny as before. Use the paints to create a calm sea.

- Using a thin brush write words, describing a calm sea, as gentle waves.

Robbers

There are many things in life which rob people of their peace of mind: worry, poverty, illness, arguments. All these things upset us, and rob us of our peace.

Read the story of "The Ten Lepers", page 32.

What robbed the people suffering from leprosy of their peace?

Read the passage "The Flowers of the Field", Book 1, page 37.

How does worry rob people of their peace of mind?

Activity

• Discuss with a friend other things which rob people of their peace. Make a list of your suggestions. When you have done this, draw some burglars. On their T–shirts write the names of things that rob people of their peace of mind. Underneath your burglars, write some suggestions for helping to restore lost peace of mind.

• Look up Jesus' advice about worry in Matthew 6.34.

A Coat Hanger

A coat hanger poem is one in which the subject of the poem is written down the middle of the page and the line is written either side.

Activity

- Write the word "Peace" down the middle of your page in coloured pencil.

- Write a five line poem about peace.

  The first line must have a P in it.
  The second line must have an E in it, etc.

  The coloured letters do not have to come exactly in the middle.

- Your poem can be based on any of the stories about peace, or you can write about peace in general. This poem is based on Noah, page 45.

Example:

The dove of Peace
Rests its tirEd wings
The olive brAnch
Lays Crumpled on the deck
As Noah strokEs the weary bird.

GIFTS

Understanding the biblical ideas

Christians believe that life is full of gifts from God. Life itself is a gift, as is the world around us. They believe Jesus was a gift from God, sent with love — a surprise Christmas present for the world. Many people in the first century were looking for a special king but some expected a warrior or a powerful leader, not a baby born to poor parents.

The gift of Jesus reflects for Christians both God's love and the world's need. They believe Jesus came to fulfil a purpose just as ordinary gifts often fulfil a need. They believe Jesus came to put right the wrong in the world and bring people back into friendship with God.

Traditionally the wise men's gifts have been seen as symbolic. Gold was for a king. Frankincense was for a priest. Myrrh was a sign of suffering. It was used in burial and it was also a painkiller (although in the Old Testament it is often used for celebration). Myrrh was offered to Jesus when he was on the cross, but he refused it.

Jesus made it plain that giving to others counted as giving to him: "Whoever welcomes one of these children in my name, welcomes me." See also the parable of "The Sheep and the Goats", Book 3, page 18.

Giving should cost. Giving left overs is not enough. David was offered the ground for the Temple free but he insisted on paying. He said to the owner, "I will not offer to God that which cost me nothing." It was for this reason that the widow who gave two small coins was praised, for she had given all she had. Hannah gave the most precious thing she had — Samuel — in response to the gift God had given her — her child.

People can give to God in response to his gifts. Giving can be of love, worship, time, money, talent, and oneself. Whatever is given, it is only giving back to God that which God gave in the first place. Christians acknowledge this when they say, "All things come from you, O Lord, and of your own have we given you."

Introducing the passages

Discuss presents with the children. Explore the following aspects: choosing appropriate presents, surprise presents, unwanted presents, the different ways we respond to presents, non–material presents, presents with a meaning.

The story of Christmas is about Jesus being a surprise present and people responding to him in various ways.

Explore presents with a meaning with children. The wise men's presents were symbolic — they each had a meaning.

The story of Hannah's present is about value and gratitude. When do we say thank you for presents and how do we say it? Hannah showed her gratitude in an unusual way.

The story of "The Man at the Gate" is about a gift often taken for granted — health.

Other useful passages

The whole group entitled "Sharing", Book 1, page 63–69.

The gift of forgiveness, Book 1, pages 78–83.

"Solomon's invisible gift", page 4.

Any of the miracle stories could be included under the theme of the gift of healing: pages 32, 36, 103; Book 1, page 8.

The gifts of the Holy Spirit can be found under "Understanding the Holy Spirit", Book 3, page 97.

The gift of the Law can be found under the section entitled "Laws for Living", pages 18–22.

The rest of the Christmas story can be found in Book 3, page 8.

Cross–curricular links

English
- Write a story about a surprise present or the gift you would most like to give/receive. It need not be a material gift but a talent or invisible quality. (2)
- Look at the giving and receiving of letters — some are more popular than others (bills, invitations, etc.) Write a variety of letters for different purposes/audiences. (2, 3)
- Discuss the saying "Giving is better than receiving." (1)
- Explore some of the inventions/discoveries made by famous scientists and the "gifts" they gave to the world: Marie Curie — radiation, Louis Pasteur — Pasteurisation. (2)
- Turn the story of Hannah into a short "radio play" using a cassette. (1)

Mathematics
- Imagine you have twenty pounds. Use a catalogue from a chain store and plan buying gifts for your family or friends. Calculate the cost. (1, 2)
- Giving to charity: if we gave 10p a week how much would that be for the class, year group, or school for a month or a year? (1, 2)

Geography
- Investigate what it costs to send presents of a certain weight to various places in the UK. Plot the places, prices, and distances on a map.

Music
- Create a Christmas song in the form of a lullaby. Listen to the carol "Lullay my Liking." (*The Oxford Book of Carols*). (1)
- Listen to the various ways the Christmas story has been expressed in song throughout the ages. This can be done using a good hymn book with the accompanying music book. (2)

Personal and Social Education
- Talk about giving to charity. Use promotional literature to find out what can be bought with the money given. Is it a surprise how little it costs to have an eye cataract removed? What is our responsibility when it costs us so little to give someone back their sight or pure water, etc.? (EAT 1)

Science
- Design a card with a moving part which can accompany a gift at Christmas or some other occasion when gifts are given. (1, 4)

Technology
- Look at the various types of collecting boxes used for charitable purposes. Design a collecting box which would be attractive to children. (1, 2)
- Design and make a carton to contain and protect a small gift (e.g. a Cadbury's creme egg). Use only one sheet of A4 paper and glue. (1, 2)

Art
- Look at three different paintings of the Madonna and Child (Giotto, Fra Angelico, Holbein or any other famous artists). What do they tell us about the period when they were painted and the ideas the artist held about Mary and Jesus? (2)
- Make a collection of Christmas cards. What images of Mary and Jesus are shown on these? (2)

History
- Look at how various people have used their God–given talents and the difference they made to the world. For example: Florence Nightingale, Mary Seacole, Shaftesbury, and Martin Luther King. (1, 2, 3)

PE/Dance
- Express in mime/dance the different ways gifts are offered and received. (KS 2)

THE MAN AT THE GATE
Acts 3.1–11 ▶ *page 103*

A Christian perspective
In this story, the man is healed in Jesus' name. Peter and James do not claim that they healed him. This is in line with Old Testament thinking. When Naaman was healed, Elisha refused to accept any thank you gifts because it was God who had healed Naaman (Book 1, page 98). Christians hold the same belief today: if there is any healing of illness, it is God who does the healing, even if he uses other people.

Points of interest
1. All Jews were required to give a minimum of ten per cent of their wealth, which should have meant there was no need to beg as the poor would have been looked after. Generally the

community would have looked after local poor, and the family would also have looked after its poorer members. For sharing laws, which would have supported the poorer members of society, see Book 1, page 68.

2. In the city, the structure for looking after the poor may have broken down. The Temple would have been a good place to beg, as pious Jews would have given alms as part of their worship.

3. Peter and John, though followers of Jesus, worshipped as Jews. They were Jews who acknowledged Jesus as their Messiah. Christians continued this practice until persecution caused them to separate from the Jewish community.

HANNAH'S PRECIOUS GIFT
1 Samuel 1–2.11 ▶ *page 104*

A Christian perspective
In this story, God gives to Hannah the gift she wants most. In response, Hannah gives to God the gift that costs her the most — Samuel. This was partly an expression of the belief that all life comes from God. The first–born son had to be "bought" back with five shekels by the parents in recognition of the belief that all people belong to God. Parents have children "on loan" and look after them for God.

Points of interest
1. Not having children was not only a great sorrow, but in those days a great shame. A woman's status went up with the birth of a child: she was then known as "mother of".

2. Making a vow was a very solemn undertaking and the vow was not to be broken. As in many societies, the spoken word had the force of law.

3. It sounds very cruel to send Samuel to live at the Temple. It would have been seen as a great honour in Hannah's society. Samuel would have stayed at home at least until he was weaned, which would have been at about three years old. What age he was when he actually started at the Temple we do not know.

4. In the wilderness, the Israelites had a portable tent–Temple. Here, they seem to have a more permanent structure. Israelites went to the Temple for three great feasts a year. This was probably one of those occasions.

THE WIDOW'S GIFT
Luke 21.1–4 ▶ *page 105*

A Christian perspective
The widow's gift was considered great by God because it was all she had. Christians believe giving should cost in some way. Giving out of surplus does not count.

Points of interest
1. A widow, particularly if she had no son, was in a very precarious position. To give away what little she had was courage and faith indeed.

2. The widow offered two of the smallest coins, two lepta.

3. The offering boxes were like large upturned trumpets where people contributed funds to build and repair the Temple. There were thirteen of them situated in the Women's Court.

4. This Temple was started by Herod the Great — the Herod who tried to kill Jesus when he was a baby. It was only finished about AD 64. When the building work was eventually finished, it meant 18,000 jobs came to an end. It was destroyed six years later by the Romans!

THE WISE MEN'S GIFTS
CHRISTMAS: EPISODE 3
Matthew 1.18–2.12 ▶ *page 106*

A Christian perspective
The writer is pointing out that even at his birth some people recognized Jesus as a king. Throughout the story, there is the theme of God guiding and protecting — first through the star, then the dream. The prophet, of whom Herod's wise men spoke, was Micah. Bethlehem was the home of King David. It was expected that the Messiah or special king would be a descendant of David. This would have bothered Herod, as a Davidic king would have a better claim to the throne than he had. Herod was only half Jewish. Christians believe Jesus was that special king.

Points of interest
1. Herod, known as Herod the Great, was ruthless. He killed his own wife and several of his own children, beside countless ordinary people. He was terrified of plots against him. The incident of the slaughter of the babies which follows on from this story would fit with his character.

2. The wise men, not kings, came from the East, from the area of Babylon/Persia, modern Iraq/Iran. In these areas, wise men had made many discoveries in the areas of maths and

astronomy. Like Egypt and the Indus valley this was one of the early centres of civilization.

3. The gifts have traditionally been given the following meanings: gold — a gift for king; frankincense — a gift for a priest: it was used in worship in the temple; myrrh for suffering. Myrrh was a painkiller and used to embalm dead bodies. Myrrh was also, ironically, a symbol of joy in the Old Testament, as it was a perfume. All the gifts came from Arabia but were available all over the Middle East.

5. Herod died in 4 BC so Jesus was probably born about 6 BC.

THE GIFT OF JESUS
CHRISTMAS: EPISODE 2
Luke 2.1–20 ▶ *page 107*

A Christian perspective
Christians believe Jesus was the long–awaited Messiah or Christ (anointed one). The Jews had been expecting the Messiah or Christ for many years, but some expected him to be a great leader or warrior, not a baby born in poverty. For these, Jesus was an unexpected present. Jesus (the name means "God saves") was born into an ordinary family. Christians believe he is God's son, who experienced ordinary human life.

Points of interest
1. Hired shepherds were a disreputable group: their word was not accepted in court. It was to these outcasts that the news of Jesus' birth was sent — just as, later, the news of the resurrection was given to a woman, whose testimony was equally unacceptable.

2. We do not know if Jesus was born in a stable. The text says he was laid in a manger, an animal feeding trough, therefore people have assumed it was in a stable. He could have been born in a stable, in a cave used as a stable, or in the home of a poor family. In such homes, the animals shared the lower part of the house with the family. It may be that Joseph and Mary stayed at the house of a relative, but found the guest room occupied and therefore had to share the downstairs room with the animals. Mangers were used as cradles sometimes. Woollen hammocks were also used.

3. Mary wrapped Jesus in swaddling bands, the standard treatment for the day. The baby was wrapped in a large cloth which was secured with bands, sometimes embroidered. Mary did this herself, which may mean she had no help at the birth. The baby would also have been rubbed with salt and olive oil.

4. The date of Jesus' birth was probably about 6 BC. No evidence has been found yet of a worldwide census around that time, but Rome regularly conducted enrolments for taxation. One of these took place about 8 BC and could have taken some time to complete, as such surveys often did in the ancient world.

5. Sometimes inns were private houses with a guest room. There were also lodging places where animals could be sheltered overnight and the owners could find a place to rest.

The Man at the Gate

Acts 3.1—11

The man looked up at Peter and John. What were they going to give him? He held up his hands hopefully. But Peter and John did not place any money or food in them. They looked at him, longing to help. He came here to the Temple to beg. He couldn't walk and so couldn't earn any money. Peter and John knew that God wanted to give this man a much better gift than money. Peter spoke to him. "I don't have any money to give you, but I do have a greater gift for you. By Jesus' power, stand up and walk." Peter leaned down and grasped the man's hand. He helped him to stand up! The man was amazed to realize that his ankles and feet were suddenly strong enough to support him. He was healed! He was so overjoyed that he began to walk, then to run and then to jump! His ankles were fine. He hurried back to the Temple with Peter and John. He clung on to Peter's arm.

"Tell me more about this Jesus," he said.

The other people watching him were amazed. They were used to seeing him begging, not running around. Who were these two men? How had they been able to do this incredible thing? They crowded round Peter and John: they must find out more, too.

Hannah's Precious Gift

1 Samuel 1—2.11

Hannah was so unhappy! She wanted to have a baby so much! After tea, she left the rest of her family, and went into the special Temple to be alone with God and to beg him to answer her prayer: "O God, please let me have a baby!" There in the Temple she thought about Elkanah, her husband. He was a good man, always telling her that he loved her, but still Hannah longed for a child. Some women were not so kind! They made fun of her — as if it were her fault she had no baby to love. "Dear God," Hannah prayed, "if you give me a son, I promise that I will bring him up to love and serve you. When he is old enough I will bring him here to your Temple, to live."

Now while Hannah prayed, the priest, Eli, was watching her. He thought she was behaving very strangely, for she was praying silently, but moving her lips for the words, and she was crying very bitterly. In the end, he went up to her thinking she was drunk. "This is no way to behave here in God's house!" he said. "Control yourself."

Hannah was startled. She looked up at him. "But I'm only praying!" she explained. "I am very unhappy and I came to ask God for his help."

Eli looked at her. He could see how sad she was. Her eyes were red, and she looked pale and tired. He spoke more kindly to her. "Go home now, and stop worrying about it — God knows how unhappy you are. I pray that he will give you what you need."

Hannah felt better. She thanked Eli, and went back to her husband. Soon it was time for the family to return home from that year's visit to the special Temple. When she had been at home a few weeks, Hannah realized that God had answered her prayer: she was going to have a baby. How happy she was! She began to get clothes ready for the baby, and her husband was pleased to see his wife happy and busy. Together they began to count the days until they would see their child.

When the baby was born, it was the son Hannah had prayed for. She called him Samuel. Now she explained to Elkanah how she had asked God to give her this child. She described the promise she had made about him. Her husband listened. He would be sorry for Samuel to live so far away from them. He knew that Hannah would miss him too. But he knew that she must keep her promise. After all, the boy was God's gift to them. They must give him back to God when he was old enough to leave home.

So, as soon as Samuel was old enough, Hannah packed up his clothes, and they travelled to the Temple, where he would live. Eli the priest would look after him and would teach him all he needed to know. Hannah and Elkanah said goodbye to their son and left him at the Temple. They visited Samuel regularly, and thanked God for this special gift of a child.

RESOURCE BANK 2: GIFTS

The Widow's Gift

Luke 21.1–4

The Women's Court at the Temple was a busy place. Sometimes choirs sang from its steps. Usually, there were many moneychangers working there, and stallkeepers selling articles the people needed in their worship of God. A steady stream of men passed through it on their way to the Inner Courts. Also there were the offering boxes, for people's money gifts to God. Around the edges of the Court were small groups of people discussing religious issues, or being taught by one of the religious leaders.

Jesus himself often taught here, where women as well as men could hear him. One day, as he talked to his listeners, he was aware of the different people coming into the Court to bring their offerings. He saw rich men, proud of their generosity, openly carrying purses jangling with gold coins. They made sure that everyone else could see how heavy their purses were, and could catch the gleam of gold as the coins dropped into the boxes. They even looked round, to make sure people were watching. "Everyone must be thinking how good and generous I am!" they thought. They stalked off, full of their own importance.

But Jesus saw other, very different people, come too. He watched the poor people come into the Court, quietly dropping in the few coins they could afford to give. One woman in particular caught his attention. He pointed her out to his listeners.

"Look," he said quietly. "That woman over there is a widow. She has just put in two of the smallest coins we have. I have watched some rich men today giving many gold coins. But I tell you this: that woman has given to God far more than they have. They could easily afford to give much money. She has given everything she has because she loves God."

The Wise Men's Gifts

CHRISTMAS: EPISODE 3

Matthew 1.18—2.12

It had been a long, hard journey. They had been travelling for so long and the roads were so bad. Their animals were tired, and they were tired. Now, as they got near to Jerusalem, they were sure that, finally, they were where they should be. "This is the capital city," one of them said. "Surely the new King of the Jews will be here."

"Yes," another one agreed. "We've arrived at last. The star has led us well. We don't need it now. Let's find the great king we've read about at home."

They entered the city and began to ask people, "Where is the new King of the Jews?" They had thought that everyone there would be full of the news, but no one could help them at all. King Herod, in the palace, heard about these rich strangers, asking questions in his city. "What do they mean, a new king? I am the king. Who are they?"

"We're not sure," his advisers said. "They seem to be rich, and they've come a long way. The prophets wrote that the great king, the Messiah, will be born in Bethlehem. Perhaps that is whom they are looking for."

Herod was worried. He was the king. No one else must be allowed to take over! He sent for the travellers secretly. He pretended to be friendly and helpful. He must find out where the "king" was.

"I'm sorry, the new king isn't here," he said craftily. " My advisers tell me that the prophets say that he will be born in the little town of Bethlehem. I hope you will find him. Do come back and tell me just where he's living because I would like to see him, too."

So the travellers left the palace. They had made a terrible mistake. The star was still there. It had been leading them not to Jerusalem, but through Jerusalem, on to Bethlehem. Now they realized that it was not shining over this city. They followed it again, on and on. This time they noted carefully just where the star was. It led them to Bethlehem and there they found where Joseph and Mary were living. Wearily they dug out the presents they had brought. They looked at the house. Surely a great king wouldn't be here? But they'd been wrong once, when they thought they knew best. They went inside. There they found, not a king in rich clothes, surrounded by servants, but an ordinary family — a mother, a father, and a small boy. So this was God's special king. They knelt in front of him and worshipped him. They gave his mother and father their gifts for him — gifts not suitable for this little boy yet. There was frankincense, gold, and there was myrrh, a rich spice. Mary thought about these gifts. Dimly, she knew what each one meant. Then she busied herself finding somewhere for the travellers to sleep.

As they slept, God warned them in a dream that Herod wanted only to kill the child. They must go back to their own country another way, avoiding Jerusalem. So they set off on the long journey home.

The Gift of Jesus
CHRISTMAS: EPISODE 2

Luke 2.1–20

It was cold on the hills around Bethlehem during the nights. The men who stayed up there to look after their sheep huddled round their fires. That night was like any other out there in the loneliness of the hills. The men watched while the last gleams of lamplight disappeared, down in the village. From time to time they left the fire, walking round the flock to make sure all was well. Even here, near the village, there were wild animals who would come to steal an easy meal among the drowsy sheep. Sometimes the shepherds sang quietly, to comfort themselves and their animals. Sometimes they told each other stories. Always the nights were long and cold and dark.

Tonight, though, the darkness was suddenly broken. Bright warm light flooded their camp, reflecting in the eyes of the startled sheep around them. The men staggered to their feet, shielding their faces from the brightness. What was happening? It was as if the sun was shining on them! As their eyes grew accustomed to the light, they realized that there was a figure in front of them, a man whose face and clothes shone with brightness. They were terrified! But the stranger spoke to them, urgently. "No, don't be frightened!" he told them. "I've come to tell you some good news — good news for everyone. A baby has just been born, tonight, down in Bethlehem. He is the special king we have been waiting for, the Lord. He has come to tell everyone that God loves them. Listen! This special baby is lying in an animal's feeding trough. When you find him there, you will know that I am telling you the truth. Hurry now, and go to him."

As soon as he'd finished speaking, he was surrounded by many other radiant figures. The shepherds listened in amazement as their visitors sang beautiful songs of praise to God:

> "Glory to God in the highest
> And on earth, peace, to men of goodwill."

Suddenly, all was quiet again, and darkness was everywhere once more.

"We must go — now — to Bethlehem," one of the shepherds shouted, breaking the silence. "God himself has sent his angels to tell us about this baby. Come on quickly!"

Down in Bethlehem, in a rough shelter in which the owners kept their animals, there was a baby, lying peacefully asleep in a manger. His young mother and her husband had carefully wrapped him up in swaddling bands. They had padded the trough with clean hay, and had settled down their precious little baby. Mary, his mother, lay exhausted on a pile of straw, Joseph's cloak over her. It had been such a long, difficult journey from their home in Nazareth — all just to have their names registered here in Bethlehem, where Joseph's family had come from. And then they had found no comfortable inn to stay in. Finally, someone had said they could sleep here — in the stable! But Mary had been too tired and desperate to argue. Joseph had done his best to clean out the stable: it was at least dry and fairly warm after their long journey. And it was quiet and private. Here, Mary had given birth to Jesus.

She raised her head to gaze at his small face yet again. He looked so fragile, so vulnerable, and — even though she thought him the most beautiful baby in the world — so ordinary.

Advent Garland

For many years, the Israelites had waited for a special king. Christians believe Jesus was that king.

Before Christmas, Christians celebrate Advent. This is a time of getting ready, of remembering that on that first Christmas Jesus was not welcomed. Not many people knew he had been born, and not many people thought he was the special king. There was no room at the inn and Jesus was born in a stable.

During Advent, Christians think about the coming of Jesus, and how he was homeless and unwelcomed. They try to make sure that as Christians they welcome Jesus in their hearts.

Activity

- In India, visitors are often welcomed with a garland. Welcome garlands can be used as a Christmas decoration to express the idea of welcoming Jesus. Make flowers from tissue and thread them on a string. Make the string long enough to go over a person's head.

- When your garlands are finished hang them as decorations. Write the word "welcome" on coloured pieces of paper in many different languages and scripts. Display these words in between the garlands.

Jesus is Born

Read "The Gift of Jesus" on page 107.

When Jesus was born, he was wrapped in swaddling bands. In those days, babies were washed and rubbed with salt and oil, and wrapped in a large piece of material which was then tied with bands of cloth to hold it in place.

Sometimes the bands were beautifully embroidered. The baby was then hung in a woollen hammock between two sticks, or from two beams, or carried on the mother's back.

Christians believe Jesus experienced ordinary human life. He would have been wrapped as any other baby was, carried on his mother's back or swung in a hammock. He knew what it was like to be a child.

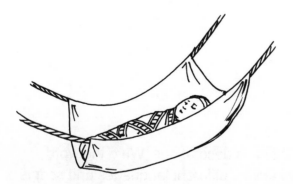

Because Jesus experienced human life, Christians believe they can pray to him knowing he understands.

Activity

- Try wrapping a baby doll in swaddling bands in the traditional manner. You will need a square of white sheeting and some wide, coloured braid.

- You might also like to design a simple hammock for the baby.

The Man at the Gate

Read the story of "The Man at the Gate" on page 103.

Giving was essential for all Jews. They gave a minimum of one tenth of their wealth. The poor were the responsibility of the rich. If a person had wealth, it was theirs to share. Giving one tenth is known as "tithing". This practice is still carried on in many churches. In medieval times, tithes of farm produce were collected in special barns called "tithe barns".

Group activity

- Are there any tithe barns in your area?

- Think about your pocket money, if you have any. What would one tenth be?

- Giving to those in need used to be known as "alms giving". Find out what the word "alms" means.

- Are there any "alms houses" in your area?

- Find out what an "almoner" was.

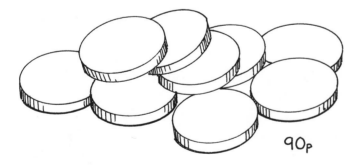

90p

10p

Think about it

Peter and John gave more than they were asked. The man asked for alms. They, in Jesus' name, tackled the source of the problem.

Writing Backwards

Read the story of "Hannah's Precious Gift" on page 104.

Not all stories start at the beginning and end at the end. Sometimes a book starts at the end of a story and the character remembers what happened earlier. Some stories are full of these "flashbacks".

Activity

• Look at the writing below. Imagine it is written by Hannah when she was older. Her son, Samuel, is grown up. Complete the story.

   Hannah looked up at her son. Although not very tall he was still a head taller than she was. Hannah could hardly believe he was twenty now; it seemed no time since…

Think about it

Hannah gave the most precious gift she had — Samuel — because she believed God had given him to her in the first place.